GENESIS

The First Book of Moses

This **WORKBOOK** is designed to help assist the diligent study of those who would know the Word of God. It is written in a format that **REQUIRES** reading of the text from the Authorized King James Version of the Holy Scriptures.

The King James Bible correctly fills all of the available "blanks" in this workbook.

Other workbooks are available by contacting us:

By FAITH Publications
85 Hendersonville Hwy.
Walterboro, SC 29488

(843) 538-2269

<u>**www.faithbaptistchurch.us**</u>

publications@faithbaptistchurch.us

Genesis 1:1-50:26

In the beginning _____ _____ the heaven and the earth. ²And the earth was without form, and void; and darkness *was* upon the face of the deep. And the Spirit of God moved upon the face of the waters.

³And God _____ , Let there be light: and there was light. ⁴And God saw the light, that *it was* good: and God divided the light from the darkness. ⁵And God called the light Day, and the darkness he called Night. And the evening and the morning were the _____ day.

⁶And God said, Let there be a firmament in the midst of the waters, and let it divide the waters from the waters. ⁷And God made the firmament, and divided the waters which *were* under the firmament from the waters which *were* above the firmament: and it was so. ⁸And God called the firmament _____ . And the evening and the morning were the _____ day.

⁹And God said, Let the waters under the heaven be gathered together unto one place, and let the dry *land* appear: and it was so. ¹⁰And God called the dry *land* _____ ; and the gathering together of the waters called he _____ : and God saw that *it was* good. ¹¹And God said, Let the earth bring forth grass, the herb yielding seed, *and* the fruit tree yielding fruit after his kind, whose seed *is* in itself, upon the earth: and it was so. ¹²And the earth brought forth grass, *and* herb yielding seed after his kind, and the tree yielding fruit, whose seed *was* in itself, after his kind: and God saw that *it was* good. ¹³And the evening and the morning were the _____ day.

¹⁴And God said, Let there be lights in the firmament of the heaven to divide the day from the night; and let them be for _____ , and for _____ , and for _____ , and _____ : ¹⁵And let them be for _____ in the firmament of the heaven to give _____ upon the earth: and it was so. ¹⁶And God made two great lights; the greater light to rule the day, and the lesser light to rule the night: *he made* the stars also. ¹⁷And God set them in the firmament of the heaven to give light upon the earth, ¹⁸And to rule over the day and over the night, and to divide the light from the darkness: and God saw that *it was* good. ¹⁹And the evening and the morning were the _____ day. ²⁰And God said, Let the waters bring forth abundantly the moving creature that hath life, and fowl *that* may fly above the earth in the open firmament of heaven. ²¹And God created great whales, and every living creature that moveth, which the waters brought forth abundantly, after their kind, and every winged fowl after his kind: and God saw that *it was* good. ²²And God blessed them, saying, Be fruitful, and multiply, and fill the waters in the seas, and let fowl multiply in the earth. ²³And the evening and the morning were the _____ day.

²⁴And God said, Let the earth bring forth the living creature after his kind, cattle, and creeping thing, and beast of the earth after his kind: and it was so. ²⁵And God made the beast of the earth after his kind, and cattle after their kind, and every thing that creepeth upon the earth after his kind: and God saw that *it was* good.

²⁶And God said, Let us make _____ in _____ image, after our likeness: and let them have dominion over the fish of the sea, and over the fowl of the air, and over the cattle, and over all the earth, and over every creeping thing that creepeth upon the earth. ²⁷So _____ _____ _____ in his *own* _____ , in the image of _____ created he him; _____ and _____ created he them. ²⁸And God _____ them, and God said unto them, Be fruitful, and multiply, and replenish the earth, and subdue it:

and have dominion over the fish of the sea, and over the fowl of the air, and over every living thing that moveth upon the earth.

²⁹And God said, Behold, I have given you every herb bearing seed, which *is* upon the face of all the earth, and every tree, in the which *is* the fruit of a tree yielding seed; to you it shall be for meat. ³⁰And to every beast of the earth, and to every fowl of the air, and to every thing that creepeth upon the earth, wherein *there is* life, *I have given* every green herb for meat: and it was so. ³¹And God saw every thing that he had made, and, behold, *it was* _____ _____. And the evening and the morning were the _____ day.

²:¹Thus the heavens and the earth were finished, and all the host of them. ²And on the seventh day God ended his work which he had made; and he _____ on the _____ day from all his work which he had made. ³And God blessed the seventh day, and sanctified it: because that in it he had rested from all his work which God created and made.

⁴These *are* the generations of the heavens and of the earth when they were created, in the day that the LORD God made the earth and the heavens, ⁵And every plant of the field before it was in the earth, and every herb of the field before it grew: for the LORD God had not caused it to rain upon the earth, and *there was* not a man to till the ground. ⁶But there went up a mist from the earth, and watered the whole face of the ground. ⁷And the LORD God formed man *of* the _____ of the ground, and breathed into his nostrils the breath of life; and _____ became a _____ _____.

⁸And the LORD God planted a garden eastward in Eden; and there he put the man whom he had formed. ⁹And out of the ground made the LORD God to grow every tree that is pleasant to the sight, and good for food; the tree of _____ also in the midst of the garden, and the tree of _____ of _____ and _____. ¹⁰And a river went out of Eden to water the garden; and from thence it was parted, and became into four heads. ¹¹The name of the first *is* Pison: that *is* it which compasseth the whole land of Havilah, where *there is* gold; ¹²And the gold of that land *is* good: there *is* bdellium and the onyx stone. ¹³And the name of the second river *is* Gihon: the same *is* it that compasseth the whole land of Ethiopia. ¹⁴And the name of the third river *is* Hiddekel: that *is* it which goeth toward the east of Assyria. And the fourth river *is* Euphrates. ¹⁵And the LORD God took the man, and put him into the garden of Eden to dress it and to keep it. ¹⁶And the LORD God commanded the man, saying, Of every tree of the garden thou mayest freely eat: ¹⁷But of the tree of the knowledge of good and evil, thou shalt _____ eat of it: for in the day that thou eatest thereof thou shalt _____ _____.

¹⁸And the LORD God said, *It is* _____ good that the man should be _____; I will make him an _____ _____ for him. ¹⁹And out of the ground the LORD God formed every beast of the field, and every fowl of the air; and brought *them* unto Adam to see what he would call them: and whatsoever Adam called every living creature, that *was* the name thereof. ²⁰And Adam gave names to all cattle, and to the fowl of the air, and to every beast of the field; but for Adam there was not found an _____ meet for him. ²¹And the LORD God caused a deep sleep to fall upon Adam and he slept: and he took one of his _____, and closed up the flesh instead thereof; ²²And the rib, which the LORD God had taken from man, made he a woman, and brought her unto the man. ²³And Adam said, This *is* now bone of my bones, and flesh of my flesh: she shall be called _____, because she was taken out of Man. ²⁴Therefore shall a _____ leave his father and his

mother, and shall _____ unto his wife: and they shall be _____ _____. ²⁵And they were both naked, the man and his wife, and were not ashamed.

³:¹Now the serpent was more subtil than any beast of the field which the LORD God had made. And he said unto the woman, Yea, _____ God said, Ye shall not eat of every tree of the garden?

²And the woman said unto the serpent, We may eat of the fruit of the trees of the garden: ³But of the fruit of the tree which *is* in the midst of the garden, God hath said, Ye shall not eat of it, neither shall ye touch it, lest ye die. ⁴And the serpent said unto the woman, Ye shall _____ surely die: ⁵For God doth know that in the day ye eat thereof, then your eyes shall be opened, and ye shall be _____ gods, _____ _____ and _____. ⁶And when the woman saw that the tree *was* good for _____, and that it *was* pleasant to the _____, and a tree to be desired to make *one* _____, she took of the fruit thereof, and did _____, and gave also unto her husband with her; and he did _____. ⁷And the eyes of them both were opened, and they knew that they *were* naked; and they sewed fig leaves together, and made themselves aprons. ⁸And they heard the _____ of the LORD God _____ in the garden in the cool of the day: and Adam and his wife hid themselves from the presence of the LORD God amongst the trees of the garden. ⁹And the LORD God called unto Adam, and said unto him, Where *art* thou? ¹⁰And he said, I heard thy _____ in the garden, and I was afraid, because I *was* naked; and I hid myself. ¹¹And he said, Who told thee that thou *wast* naked? Hast thou eaten of the tree, whereof I commanded thee that thou shouldest not eat? ¹²And the man said, The woman whom thou gavest *to be* with me, she gave me of the tree, and ____ _____ eat. ¹³And the LORD God said unto the woman, What *is* this *that* thou hast done? And the woman said, The serpent _____ me, and I did eat. ¹⁴And the LORD God said unto the serpent, Because thou hast done this, thou *art* cursed above all cattle, and above every beast of the field; upon thy belly shalt thou go, and dust shalt thou eat all the days of thy life: ¹⁵And I will put enmity between thee and the woman, and between thy seed and _____ seed; it shall bruise thy head, and thou shalt bruise _____ heel. ¹⁶Unto the woman he said, I will greatly multiply thy sorrow and thy conception; in sorrow thou shalt bring forth children; and thy _____ *shall be* to thy _____, and he shall _____ over thee. ¹⁷And unto Adam he said, Because thou hast hearkened unto the voice of thy wife, and hast eaten of the tree, of which I commanded thee, saying, Thou shalt not eat of it: cursed *is* the ground for thy sake; in sorrow shalt thou eat *of* it all the days of thy life; ¹⁸Thorns also and thistles shall it bring forth to thee; and thou shalt eat the herb of the field; ¹⁹In the sweat of thy face shalt thou eat bread, till thou return unto the ground; for out of it wast thou taken: for dust thou *art,* and unto dust shalt thou return. ²⁰And Adam called his wife's name _____; because she was the mother of _____ living. ²¹Unto Adam also and to his wife did the LORD God make coats of skins, and clothed them. ²²And the LORD God said, Behold, the man is become as one of us, to know good and evil: and now, lest he put forth his hand, and take also of the tree of life, and eat, and live for ever: ²³Therefore the LORD God sent him forth from the garden of Eden, to till the ground from whence he was taken. ²⁴So he drove out the man; and he placed at the east of the garden of Eden Cherubim, and a flaming sword which turned every way, to keep the way of the tree of life.

⁴:¹And Adam knew Eve his wife; and she conceived, and bare _____, and said, I have gotten a man from the LORD. ²And she again bare his brother _____. And Abel

was a keeper of _____, but Cain was a _____ of the _____. ³And in process of time it came to pass, that Cain brought of the _____ of the _____ an offering unto the LORD. ⁴And Abel, he also brought of the _____ of his _____ and of the fat thereof. And the LORD had _____ unto _____ and to his offering: ⁵But unto _____ and to his offering he had _____ respect. And Cain was very wroth, and his _____ fell. ⁶And the LORD said unto Cain, Why art thou wroth? and why is thy _____ fallen? ⁷If thou _____ _____, shalt thou not be _____? and if thou _____ _____ _____, _____ lieth at the _____. And unto thee *shall be* his desire, and thou shalt rule over him. ⁸And Cain talked with Abel his brother: and it came to pass, when they were in the field, that Cain rose up against Abel his brother, and _____ him.

⁹And the LORD said unto Cain, Where *is* Abel thy brother? And he said, I know not: *Am* I my _____ _____? ¹⁰And he said, _____ hast thou _____? the _____ of thy brother's _____ crieth unto me from the ground. ¹¹And now *art* thou _____ from the earth, which hath opened her mouth to receive thy brother's blood from thy hand; ¹²When thou tillest the ground, it shall not henceforth yield unto thee her strength; a fugitive and a vagabond shalt thou be in the earth. ¹³And Cain said unto the LORD, My punishment *is* greater than I can bear. ¹⁴Behold, thou hast driven me out this day from the face of the earth; and from thy face shall I be hid; and I shall be a fugitive and a vagabond in the earth; and it shall come to pass, *that* every one that findeth me shall slay me. ¹⁵And the LORD said unto him, Therefore whosoever slayeth Cain, vengeance shall be taken on him _____. And the LORD set a _____ upon Cain, lest any finding him should kill him.

¹⁶And Cain went out from the presence of the LORD, and dwelt in the land of Nod, on the east of Eden. ¹⁷And Cain knew his wife; and she conceived, and bare _____: and he builded a city, and called the name of the city, after the name of his son, Enoch. ¹⁸And unto Enoch was born _____: and Irad begat _____: and Mehujael begat _____: and Methusael begat _____.

¹⁹And Lamech took unto him _____ _____: the name of the one *was* Adah, and the name of the other Zillah. ²⁰And Adah bare Jabal: he was the father of such as dwell in tents, and *of such as have* cattle. ²¹And his brother's name *was* Jubal: he was the father of all such as handle the harp and organ. ²²And Zillah, she also bare Tubal-cain, an instructer of every artificer in brass and iron: and the sister of Tubal-cain *was* Naamah. ²³And Lamech said unto his wives, Adah and Zillah, Hear my voice; ye wives of Lamech, hearken unto my speech: for I have slain a man to my wounding, and a young man to my hurt. ²⁴If Cain shall be avenged sevenfold, truly Lamech seventy and sevenfold.

²⁵And Adam knew his wife again; and she bare a son, and called his name _____: For _____, *said she,* hath _____ me another _____ instead of _____, whom _____ slew. ²⁶And to Seth, to him also there was born a son; and he called his name _____: _____ began men to _____ upon the _____ of the _____.

⁵:¹This *is* the _____ of the _____ of _____. In the day that God created man, in the _____ of _____ made he him; ² _____ and _____ _____ he them; and _____ them, and called the _____ ir name Adam, in the day when they were created.

³And Adam lived an _____ and _____ years, and begat *a son* in his own likeness, after his image; and called his name _____: ⁴And the days of Adam after he

had begotten Seth were _____ hundred years: and he begat sons and daughters: ⁵And all the days that Adam lived were _____ hundred and _____ years: and he _____. ⁶And Seth lived an hundred and _____ years, and begat Enos: ⁷And Seth lived after he begat Enos _____ hundred and _____ years, and begat sons and daughters: ⁸And all the days of Seth were _____ hundred and _____ years: and he _____.

⁹And Enos lived _____ years, and begat _____: ¹⁰And Enos lived after he begat Cainan _____ hundred and _____ years, and begat sons and daughters: ¹¹And all the days of Enos were _____ hundred and _____ years: and he _____.

¹²And Cainan lived _____ years, and begat _____: ¹³And Cainan lived after he begat Mahalaleel _____ hundred and _____ years, and begat sons and daughters: ¹⁴And all the days of Cainan were _____ hundred and _____ years: and he _____.

¹⁵And Mahalaleel lived _____ and _____ years, and begat _____: ¹⁶And Mahalaleel lived after he begat Jared _____ hundred and _____ years, and begat sons and daughters: ¹⁷And all the days of Mahalaleel were _____ hundred _____ and _____ years: and he _____.

¹⁸And Jared lived an hundred _____ and _____ years, and he begat _____: ¹⁹And Jared lived after he begat Enoch _____ hundred years, and begat sons and daughters: ²⁰And all the days of Jared were _____ hundred _____ and _____ years: and he _____.

²¹And Enoch lived _____ and _____ years, and begat _____: ²²And Enoch _____ with _____ he begat Methuselah _____ hundred years, and begat sons and daughters: ²³And all the days of Enoch were _____ hundred _____ and _____ years: ²⁴And _____ _____ _____ _____: and he *was* _____; for _____ _____ _____. ²⁵And Methuselah lived an _____ _____ and _____ years, and begat _____: ²⁶And Methuselah lived after he begat Lamech _____ hundred _____ and _____ years, and begat sons and daughters: ²⁷And all the days of Methuselah were _____ hundred _____ and _____ years: and he _____.

²⁸And Lamech lived an hundred _____ and _____ years, and begat a _____: ²⁹And he called his name _____, saying, This *same* shall _____ us concerning our _____ and _____ of our hands, because of the ground which the LORD hath cursed. ³⁰And Lamech lived after he begat Noah _____ hundred _____ and _____ years, and begat sons and daughters: ³¹And all the days of Lamech were _____ hundred _____ and _____ years: and he _____. ³²And Noah was _____ hundred years old: and Noah begat _____, _____, and _____.

⁶:¹And it came to pass, when men began to multiply on the face of the earth, and daughters were born unto them, ²That the sons of _____ saw the _____ of men that they *were* _____; and they took them wives of all which _____ chose. ³And the LORD said, My _____ shall not always _____ with man, for that he also *is* flesh: yet his days shall be an _____ and _____ years. ⁴There were _____ in the earth in those days; and also after that, when the sons of God came in unto the daughters of men, and they bare *children* to them, the same *became* _____ men which *were* of old, men of _____.

⁵And GOD saw that the _____ of man *was* _____ in the earth, and *that* every _____ of the thoughts of his heart *was* _____ _____ _____. ⁶And it repented the LORD that he had made man on the earth, and it grieved him at his _____. ⁷And the LORD said, I will destroy man whom I have created from the face of the earth; both man, and beast, and the creeping thing, and the fowls of the air; for it repenteth me that I have made them. ⁸But _____ found _____ in the eyes of the LORD.

⁹These *are* the generations of Noah: Noah was a _____ man *and* _____ in his _____, *and* Noah _____ with _____. ¹⁰And Noah begat three sons, Shem, Ham, and Japheth. ¹¹The earth also was _____ before God, and the earth was filled with _____. ¹²And God looked upon the earth, and, behold, it was corrupt; for all flesh had corrupted his way upon the earth. ¹³And God said unto Noah, The end of all flesh is come before me; for the earth is filled with violence through them; and, behold, I will _____ them with the earth.

¹⁴Make thee an _____ of gopher wood; _____ shalt thou make in the ark, and shalt _____ it _____ and _____ with pitch. ¹⁵And this *is the fashion* which thou shalt make it *of:* The _____ of the ark *shall be* _____, the _____ of it _____, and the _____ of it _____. ¹⁶A _____ shalt thou make to the ark, and in a cubit shalt thou finish it _____; and the _____ of the ark shalt thou set in the _____ thereof; *with* _____, _____, and _____ *stories* shalt thou make it. ¹⁷And, behold, I, even I, do bring a flood of waters upon the earth, to destroy all flesh, wherein *is* the _____ of life, from under heaven; *and* every thing that *is* in the earth shall die. ¹⁸But with thee will I establish my _____; and thou shalt come into the ark, thou, and thy sons, and thy wife, and thy sons' wives with thee. ¹⁹And of every living thing of all flesh, _____ of every *sort* shalt thou bring into the ark, to keep *them* alive with thee; they shall be male and female. ²⁰Of fowls after their kind, and of cattle after their kind, of every creeping thing of the earth after his kind, _____ of every *sort* shall come unto thee, to keep *them* alive. ²¹And take thou unto thee of all food that is eaten, and thou shalt gather *it* to thee; and it shall be for food for thee, and for them. ²²Thus did Noah; according to _____ that God commanded him, so _____ he.

⁷:¹And the LORD said unto Noah, Come thou and all thy house into the ark; for thee have I seen righteous before me in this generation. ²Of every _____ beast thou shalt take to thee by _____, the male and his female: and of beasts that *are* not clean by _____, the male and his female. ³Of _____ also of the air by _____, the male and the female; to keep seed alive upon the face of all the earth. ⁴For yet _____ days, and I will cause it to _____ upon the earth _____ days and _____ nights; and every living substance that I have made will I destroy from off the face of the earth. ⁵And Noah _____ according unto _____ that the LORD commanded him. ⁶And Noah *was* _____ hundred years old when the _____ of waters was upon the earth.

⁷And Noah went in, and his sons, and his wife, and his sons' wives with him, into the ark, because of the waters of the flood. ⁸Of clean beasts, and of beasts that *are* not clean, and of fowls, and of every thing that creepeth upon the earth, ⁹There went in two and two unto Noah into the ark, the male and the female, as God had commanded Noah. ¹⁰And it came to pass after seven days, that the waters of the flood were upon the earth.

GENESIS

¹¹In the six hundredth year of Noah's life, in the second month, the seventeenth day of the month, the same day were _____ _____ _____ of the great deep broken up, and the windows of heaven were opened. ¹²And the rain was upon the earth forty days and forty nights. ¹³In the selfsame day entered Noah, and Shem, and Ham, and Japheth, the sons of Noah, and Noah's wife, and the three wives of his sons with them, into the ark; ¹⁴They, and every beast after his kind, and all the cattle after their kind, and every creeping thing that creepeth upon the earth after his kind, and every fowl after his kind, every bird of every sort. ¹⁵And they went in unto Noah into the ark, two and two of all flesh, wherein *is* the _____ of _____. ¹⁶And they that went in, went in male and female of all flesh, as God had commanded him: and the _____ _____ him in. ¹⁷And the flood was forty days upon the earth; and the waters increased, and bare up the ark, and it was lift up above the earth. ¹⁸And the waters prevailed, and were increased greatly upon the earth; and the ark went upon the face of the waters. ¹⁹And the waters prevailed exceedingly upon the earth; and all the high hills, that *were* under the whole heaven, were covered. ²⁰_____ cubits upward did the waters prevail; and the _____ were _____. ²¹And all flesh _____ that moved upon the earth, both of fowl, and of cattle, and of beast, and of every creeping thing that creepeth upon the earth, and every man: ²²All in whose _____ *was* the breath of life, of all that *was* in the _____ *land,* died. ²³And every living substance was destroyed which was upon the face of the ground, both man, and cattle, and the creeping things, and the fowl of the heaven; and they were destroyed from the earth: and Noah only remained *alive,* and they that *were* with him in the ark. ²⁴And the waters prevailed upon the earth an _____ and _____ days.

⁸:¹And God _____ Noah, and every living thing, and all the cattle that *was* with him in the ark: and God made a _____ to pass over the earth, and the waters asswaged; ²The fountains also of the deep and the windows of heaven were stopped, and the rain from heaven was restrained; ³And the waters returned from off the earth continually: and after the end of the hundred and fifty days the waters were abated. ⁴And the ark rested in the seventh month, on the seventeenth day of the month, upon the mountains of _____. ⁵And the waters decreased continually until the tenth month: in the tenth *month,* on the first *day* of the month, were the tops of the mountains seen.

⁶And it came to pass at the end of forty days, that Noah opened the window of the ark which he had made: ⁷And he sent forth a _____, which went forth to and fro, until the waters were dried up from off the earth. ⁸Also he sent forth a _____ from him, to see if the waters were abated from off the face of the ground; ⁹But the dove found no _____ for the sole of her foot, and she _____ unto him into the ark, for the waters *were* on the face of the whole earth: then he put forth his hand, and took her, and pulled her in unto him _____ the _____. ¹⁰And he stayed yet other seven days; and again he sent forth the _____ out of the ark; ¹¹And the dove came in to him in the evening; and, lo, in her mouth *was* an _____ leaf pluckt off: so Noah knew that the waters were abated from off the earth. ¹²And he stayed yet other seven days; and sent forth the _____; which returned _____ again unto him any more.

¹³And it came to pass in the six hundredth and first year, in the first *month,* the first *day* of the month, the waters were dried up from off the earth: and Noah removed the covering of the ark, and looked, and, behold, the face of the ground was dry. ¹⁴And in the second month, on the seven and twentieth day of the month, was the earth dried.

GENESIS

15And God spake unto Noah, saying, 16Go forth of the ark, thou, and thy wife, and thy sons, and thy sons' wives with thee. 17Bring forth with thee every living thing that *is* with thee, of all flesh, *both* of fowl, and of cattle, and of every creeping thing that creepeth upon the earth; that they may breed abundantly in the earth, and be fruitful, and multiply upon the earth. 18And Noah went forth, and his sons, and his wife, and his sons' wives with him: 19Every beast, every creeping thing, and every fowl, *and* whatsoever creepeth upon the earth, after their kinds, went forth out of the ark.

20And Noah builded an _____ unto the LORD; and took of _____ clean beast, and of every clean fowl, and offered burnt _____ on the altar. 21And the LORD smelled a sweet savour; and the LORD said in his heart, I will _____ again curse the ground any more for man's sake; for the _____ of man's heart *is* _____ from his _____; neither will I again smite any more every thing living, as I have done. 22While the earth remaineth, _____ and _____, and _____ and _____, and _____ and _____, and _____ and _____ shall _____ cease.

9:1And God _____ Noah and his sons, and said unto them, Be fruitful, and multiply, and replenish the earth. 2And the fear of you and the dread of you shall be upon every beast of the earth, and upon every fowl of the air, upon all that moveth *upon* the earth, and upon all the fishes of the sea; into your hand are they delivered. 3Every moving thing that liveth shall be meat for you; even as the green herb have I given you all things. 4But flesh with the life thereof, *which is* the blood thereof, shall ye not eat. 5And surely your blood of your lives will I require; at the hand of every beast will I require it, and at the hand of man; at the hand of every man's brother will I require the life of man. 6Whoso _____ man's blood, by man shall his blood be shed: for in the _____ of _____ made he _____. 7And you, be ye fruitful, and multiply; bring forth abundantly in the earth, and multiply therein.

8And God spake unto Noah, and to his sons with him, saying, 9And I, behold, I establish my _____ with you, and with your seed after you; 10And with every living creature that *is* with you, of the fowl, of the cattle, and of every beast of the earth with you; from all that go out of the ark, to every beast of the earth. 11And I will establish my _____ with you; neither shall all flesh be cut off any more by the waters of a flood; neither shall there any more be a flood to destroy the earth. 12And God said, This *is* the _____ of the covenant which I make between me and you and every living creature that *is* with you, for perpetual generations: 13I do set my _____ in the _____, and it shall be for a token of a covenant between me and the earth. 14And it shall come to pass, when I bring a _____ over the earth, that the _____ shall be seen in the cloud: 15And I will _____ my covenant, which *is* between me and you and every living creature of all flesh; and the waters shall no more become a flood to destroy all flesh. 16And the bow shall be in the cloud; and I will _____ upon it, that I may _____ the everlasting covenant between God and every living creature of all flesh that *is* upon the earth. 17And God said unto Noah, This *is* the token of the covenant, which I have established between me and all flesh that *is* upon the earth.

18And the sons of Noah, that went forth of the ark, were Shem, and Ham, and Japheth: and Ham is the father of Canaan. 19These *are* the three sons of Noah: and of them was the whole earth overspread. 20And Noah began *to be* an _____, and he planted a _____: 21And he drank of the _____, and was _____; and he was _____ within his _____. 22And Ham, the father of Canaan, _____ the _____ of his father, and _____ his two brethren without. ²³And Shem and Japheth took a _____, and laid *it* upon both their _____, and went _____, and _____ the _____ of their father; and their _____ *were* _____, and they saw _____ their father's _____. ²⁴And Noah awoke from his _____, and knew what his younger son had _____ unto him. ²⁵And he said, Cursed *be* Canaan; a _____ of _____ shall he be unto his brethren. ²⁶And he said, Blessed *be* the LORD God of Shem; and Canaan shall be his _____. ²⁷God shall enlarge Japheth, and he shall dwell in the tents of Shem; and Canaan shall be his _____.

²⁸And Noah lived after the flood three hundred and fifty years. ²⁹And all the days of Noah were nine hundred and fifty years: and he _____.

¹⁰:¹Now these *are* the generations of the sons of Noah, Shem, Ham, and Japheth: and unto them were sons born after the flood. ²The sons of Japheth; _____, and _____, and Madai, and Javan, and Tubal, and Meshech, and Tiras. ³And the sons of Gomer; Ashkenaz, and Riphath, and Togarmah. ⁴And the sons of Javan; Elishah, and Tarshish, Kittim, and Dodanim. ⁵By these were the isles of the _____ divided in their lands; every one after his tongue, after their families, in their nations.

⁶And the sons of Ham; Cush, and Mizraim, and Phut, and Canaan. ⁷And the sons of Cush; Seba, and Havilah, and Sabtah, and Raamah, and Sabtechah: and the sons of Raamah; Sheba, and Dedan. ⁸And Cush begat _____: he began to be a mighty one in the earth. ⁹He was a mighty _____ before the LORD: wherefore it is said, Even as Nimrod the mighty _____ before the LORD. ¹⁰And the beginning of his kingdom was _____, and Erech, and Accad, and Calneh, in the land of _____. ¹¹Out of that land went forth Asshur, and builded _____, and the city Rehoboth, and Calah, ¹²And Resen between Nineveh and Calah: the same *is* a great city. ¹³And Mizraim begat Ludim, and Anamim, and Lehabim, and Naphtuhim, ¹⁴And Pathrusim, and Casluhim, (out of whom came _____,) and Caphtorim.

¹⁵And Canaan begat Sidon his firstborn, and Heth, ¹⁶And the Jebusite, and the Amorite, and the Girgasite, ¹⁷And the Hivite, and the Arkite, and the Sinite, ¹⁸And the Arvadite, and the Zemarite, and the Hamathite: and afterward were the families of the Canaanites spread abroad. ¹⁹And the border of the Canaanites was from Sidon, as thou comest to Gerar, unto Gaza; as thou goest, unto Sodom, and Gomorrah, and Admah, and Zeboim, even unto Lasha. ²⁰These *are* the sons of Ham, after their families, after their tongues, in their countries, *and* in their nations.

²¹Unto Shem also, the father of all the children of Eber, the brother of Japheth the elder, even to him were *children* born. ²²The children of Shem; Elam, and Asshur, and Arphaxad, and Lud, and Aram. ²³And the children of Aram; Uz, and Hul, and Gether, and Mash. ²⁴And Arphaxad begat Salah; and Salah begat Eber. ²⁵And unto Eber were born two sons: the name of one *was* Peleg; for in his days was the _____ _____; and his brother's name *was* Joktan. ²⁶And Joktan begat Almodad, and Sheleph, and Hazar-maveth, and Jerah, ²⁷And Hadoram, and Uzal, and Diklah, ²⁸And Obal, and Abimael, and Sheba, ²⁹And Ophir, and Havilah, and Jobab: all these *were* the sons of Joktan. ³⁰And their dwelling was from Mesha, as thou goest unto Sephar a mount of the east. ³¹These *are* the sons of Shem, after their families, after their tongues, in their lands, after their nations. ³²These *are* the families of the sons of Noah, after their generations, in their nations: and by these were the _____ divided in the earth after the flood.

11:1And the whole earth was of one _____, and of one _____. 2And it came to pass, as they journeyed from the east, that they found a plain in the land of _____; and they dwelt there. 3And they said one to another, Go to, let us make _____, and burn them throughly. And they had brick for _____, and slime had they for morter. 4And they said, Go to, let us _____ us a _____ and a _____, whose top *may reach* unto heaven; and let us _____ us a _____, lest we be _____ abroad upon the face of the whole earth. 5And the LORD came down to see the city and the tower, which the children of men builded. 6And the LORD said, Behold, the people *is* _____, and they have all one _____; and this they begin to do: and now nothing will be restrained from them, which they have _____ to do. 7Go to, let us go down, and there _____ their _____, that they may not understand one another's _____. 8So the LORD scattered them abroad from thence upon the face of all the earth: and they left off to build the city. 9Therefore is the name of it called _____; because the LORD did there confound the _____ of all the earth: and from thence did the _____ _____ them abroad upon the face of all the earth.

10These *are* the generations of Shem: Shem *was* an hundred years old, and begat Arphaxad two years after the flood: 11And Shem lived after he begat Arphaxad five hundred years, and begat sons and daughters. 12And Arphaxad lived five and thirty years, and begat Salah: 13And Arphaxad lived after he begat Salah four hundred and three years, and begat sons and daughters. 14And Salah lived thirty years, and begat Eber: 15And Salah lived after he begat Eber four hundred and three years, and begat sons and daughters. 16And Eber lived four and thirty years, and begat Peleg: 17And Eber lived after he begat Peleg four hundred and thirty years, and begat sons and daughters. 18And Peleg lived thirty years, and begat Reu: 19And Peleg lived after he begat Reu two hundred and nine years, and begat sons and daughters. 20And Reu lived two and thirty years, and begat Serug: 21And Reu lived after he begat Serug two hundred and seven years, and begat sons and daughters. 22And Serug lived thirty years, and begat _____: 23And Serug lived after he begat Nahor two hundred years, and begat sons and daughters. 24And Nahor lived nine and twenty years, and begat _____: 25And Nahor lived after he begat Terah an hundred and nineteen years, and begat sons and daughters. 26And Terah lived seventy years, and begat _____, _____, and _____.

27Now these *are* the generations of Terah: Terah begat Abram, Nahor, and Haran; and _____ begat _____. 28And Haran _____ _____ his father Terah in the land of his nativity, in _____ of the _____. 29And Abram and Nahor took them wives: the name of Abram's wife *was* _____; and the name of Nahor's wife, _____, the daughter of Haran, the father of Milcah, and the father of Iscah. 30But Sarai was _____; she *had* no _____. 31And Terah took Abram his son, and Lot the son of Haran his son's son, and Sarai his daughter in law, his son Abram's wife; and they went forth with them from Ur of the Chaldees, to go into the land of _____; and they came unto _____, and dwelt there. 32And the days of Terah were two hundred and five years: and Terah died in Haran.

12:1Now the LORD _____ said unto _____, Get thee _____ of thy country, and _____ thy _____, and _____ thy _____ _____, unto a _____ that _____ will _____ thee: 2And _____ _____ make of _____ a _____ _____, and I will _____ thee, and make thy _____ great; and thou shalt be a _____: 3And I will _____ them that _____ thee, and _____ him that _____ thee: and in thee shall all _____ of the earth be _____. ⁴So Abram departed, as the LORD had _____ unto him; and Lot went with him: and Abram *was* seventy and five years old when he departed out of Haran. ⁵And Abram took Sarai his wife, and Lot his brother's son, and all their substance that they had gathered, and the souls that they had gotten in Haran; and they went forth to go into the land of Canaan; and into the land of Canaan they came.

⁶And Abram passed through the land unto the place of _____, unto the plain of Moreh. And the Canaanite *was* then in the land. ⁷And the LORD appeared unto Abram, and said, Unto thy _____ will I give this _____: and there builded he an _____ unto the LORD, who appeared unto him. ⁸And he removed from thence unto a _____ on the east of _____, and pitched his tent, *having* Bethel on the west, and Hai on the east: and there he builded an altar unto the LORD, and called upon the name of the LORD. ⁹And Abram journeyed, going on still toward the south.

¹⁰And there was a famine in the land: and Abram went down into _____ to _____ there; for the famine *was* grievous in the land. ¹¹And it came to pass, when he was come near to enter into Egypt, that he said unto Sarai his wife, Behold now, I know that thou *art* a _____ woman to look upon: ¹²Therefore it shall come to pass, when the Egyptians shall see thee, that they shall say, This *is* his _____: and they will _____ me, but they will save thee alive. ¹³Say, I pray thee, thou *art* my _____: that it may be well with me for thy sake; and my soul shall live because of thee.

¹⁴And it came to pass, that, when Abram was come into Egypt, the Egyptians beheld the woman that she *was* very fair. ¹⁵The princes also of Pharaoh saw her, and commended her before Pharaoh: and the woman was taken into Pharaoh's house. ¹⁶And he entreated Abram well for her sake: and he had sheep, and oxen, and he asses, and menservants, and maidservants, and she asses, and camels. ¹⁷And the LORD _____ Pharaoh and his house with great plagues because of Sarai Abram's _____. ¹⁸And Pharaoh called Abram, and said, What *is* this *that* thou hast done unto me? why didst thou not tell me that she *was* thy wife? ¹⁹Why saidst thou, She *is* my sister? so I might have taken her to me to wife: now therefore behold thy wife, take *her,* and go thy way. ²⁰And Pharaoh commanded *his* men concerning him: and they sent him away, and his wife, and all that he had.

¹³:¹And Abram went up out of Egypt, he, and his wife, and all that he had, and Lot with him, into the south. ²And Abram *was* very _____ in cattle, in silver, and in gold. ³And he went on his journeys from the south even to Bethel, unto the place where his tent had been at the _____, between Bethel and Hai; ⁴Unto the place of the altar, which he had made there at the first: and there Abram called on the name of the LORD.

⁵And Lot also, which went with Abram, had flocks, and herds, and tents. ⁶And the land was _____ able to bear them, that they might dwell together: for their substance was great, so that they could not _____ together. ⁷And there was a _____ between the herdmen of Abram's cattle and the herdmen of Lot's cattle: and the Canaanite and the Perizzite dwelled then in the land. ⁸And Abram said unto Lot, Let there be _____ strife, I pray thee, between me and thee, and between my herdmen and thy herdmen; for we *be* _____. ⁹Is not the whole land before thee? separate thyself, I pray thee, from me: if *thou wilt take* the _____ hand, then I will go to the _____; or if *thou depart* to the right hand, then I will go to the left. ¹⁰And Lot lifted up his _____, and beheld all the plain of Jordan, that it *was* well watered every where, before the LORD destroyed

Sodom and Gomorrah, *even* as the garden of the L ORD, _____ the land of _____, as thou comest unto Zoar. [11]Then Lot _____ him all the _____ of _____; and Lot journeyed east: and they separated themselves the one from the other. [12]Abram dwelled in the land of Canaan, and Lot dwelled in the cities of the plain, and _____ *his* tent _____ _____. [13]But the men of Sodom *were* _____ and _____ before the L ORD _____.

[14]And the L ORD said unto Abram, after that Lot was separated from him, Lift up now thine eyes, and look from the place where thou art northward, and southward, and eastward, and westward: [15]For all the land which thou seest, to thee will I give it, and to thy seed for ever. [16]And I will make thy seed as the dust of the earth: so that if a man can number the dust of the earth, *then* shall thy seed also be numbered. [17]Arise, walk through the land in the length of it and in the breadth of it; for I will give it unto thee. [18]Then Abram removed *his* tent, and came and dwelt in the plain of Mamre, which *is* in Hebron, and built there an _____ unto the L ORD.

[14:1]And it came to pass in the days of Amraphel king of Shinar, Arioch king of Ellasar, Chedorlaomer king of Elam, and Tidal king of nations; [2]*That these* made war with Bera king of Sodom, and with Birsha king of Gomorrah, Shinab king of Admah, and Shemeber king of Zeboiim, and the king of Bela, which is Zoar. [3]All these were joined together in the vale of Siddim, which is the salt sea. [4]Twelve years they served Chedorlaomer, and in the thirteenth year they rebelled. [5]And in the fourteenth year came Chedorlaomer, and the kings that *were* with him, and smote the Rephaims in Ashteroth Karnaim, and the Zuzims in Ham, and the Emims in Shaveh Kiriathaim, [6]And the Horites in their mount Seir, unto El-paran, which *is* by the wilderness. [7]And they returned, and came to En-mishpat, which *is* Kadesh, and smote all the country of the Amalekites, and also the Amorites that dwelt in Hazezon-tamar. [8]And there went out the king of Sodom, and the king of Gomorrah, and the king of Admah, and the king of Zeboiim, and the king of Bela (the same *is* Zoar;) and they joined battle with them in the vale of Siddim; [9]With Chedorlaomer the king of Elam, and with Tidal king of nations, and Amraphel king of Shinar, and Arioch king of Ellasar; four kings with five. [10]And the vale of Siddim *was full of* slimepits; and the kings of Sodom and Gomorrah fled, and fell there; and they that remained fled to the mountain. [11]And they took all the goods of Sodom and Gomorrah, and all their victuals, and went their way. [12]And they took _____, Abram's brother's son, who dwelt in Sodom, and his _____, and departed.

[13]And there came one that had escaped, and told Abram the Hebrew; for he dwelt in the plain of Mamre the Amorite, brother of Eshcol, and brother of Aner: and these *were* confederate with Abram. [14]And when Abram heard that his brother was taken captive, he armed his trained *servants,* born in his own house, three hundred and eighteen, and pursued *them* unto Dan. [15]And he divided himself against them, he and his servants, by night, and smote them, and pursued them unto Hobah, which *is* on the left hand of Damascus. [16]And he brought back all the goods, and also brought again his brother Lot, and his goods, and the women also, and the people.

[17]And the _____ of _____ went out to meet him after his return from the slaughter of Chedorlaomer, and of the kings that *were* with him, at the valley of Shaveh, which *is* the king's dale. [18]And _____ king of Salem brought forth bread and wine: and he *was* the priest of the most high God. [19]And he blessed him, and said, Blessed *be* Abram of the most high God, possessor of heaven and earth: [20]And blessed be the most

high God, which hath delivered thine enemies into thy hand. And he gave him _____ of all. ²¹And the king of Sodom said unto Abram, Give me the _____, and take the _____ to thyself. ²²And Abram said to the king of Sodom, I have lift up mine hand unto the LORD, the most high God, the possessor of heaven and earth, ²³That I will _____ *take* from a _____ even to a _____, and that I will not take any _____ that *is* _____, lest thou shouldest say, I have made Abram rich: ²⁴Save only that which the young men have eaten, and the portion of the men which went with me, Aner, Eshcol, and Mamre; let them take their portion.

¹⁵:¹After these things the word of the LORD came unto Abram in a vision, saying, Fear not, Abram: I *am* thy _____, *and* thy _____ _____ _____. ²And Abram said, Lord GOD, what wilt thou _____ me, seeing I go childless, and the steward of my house is this Eliezer of Damascus? ³And Abram said, Behold, to me thou hast given no seed: and, lo, one born in my house is mine heir. ⁴And, behold, the word of the LORD *came* unto him, saying, This shall not be thine heir; but he that shall come forth out of thine own bowels shall be thine heir. ⁵And he brought him forth abroad, and said, Look now toward heaven, and tell the stars, if thou be able to number them: and he said unto him, So shall thy seed be. ⁶And he believed in the LORD; and he counted it to him for righteousness. ⁷And he said unto him, I *am* the LORD that brought thee out of Ur of the Chaldees, to give thee this land to inherit it. ⁸And he said, Lord GOD, whereby shall I know that I shall inherit it? ⁹And he said unto him, Take me an heifer of three years old, and a she goat of three years old, and a ram of three years old, and a turtledove, and a young pigeon. ¹⁰And he took unto him all these, and divided them in the midst, and laid each piece one against another: but the birds divided he not. ¹¹And when the fowls came down upon the carcases, Abram drove them away. ¹²And when the sun was going down, a deep sleep fell upon Abram; and, lo, an horror of great darkness fell upon him. ¹³And he said unto Abram, Know of a surety that thy seed shall be a stranger in a land *that is* not theirs, and shall serve them; and they shall afflict them _____ hundred years; ¹⁴And also that nation, whom they shall serve, will I _____: and afterward shall they come out with great _____. ¹⁵And thou shalt go to thy fathers in peace; thou shalt be buried in a good old age. ¹⁶But in the fourth generation they shall come hither again: for the iniquity of the Amorites *is* not yet full. ¹⁷And it came to pass, that, when the sun went down, and it was dark, behold a _____ _____, and a _____ _____ that passed between those pieces. ¹⁸In the same day the LORD made a _____ with Abram, saying, Unto thy seed have I given this _____, from the river of _____ unto the great river, the river _____: ¹⁹The Kenites, and the Kenizzites, and the Kadmonites, ²⁰And the Hittites, and the Perizzites, and the Rephaims, ²¹And the Amorites, and the Canaanites, and the Girgashites, and the Jebusites.

¹⁶:¹Now Sarai Abram's wife bare him _____ children: and she had an _____, an _____, whose name *was* _____. ²And Sarai said unto Abram, Behold now, the LORD hath restrained me from bearing: I pray thee, go in unto my maid; it may be that I may obtain children by her. And Abram hearkened to the voice of Sarai. ³And Sarai Abram's wife took Hagar her maid the Egyptian, after Abram had dwelt ten years in the land of Canaan, and gave her to her husband Abram to be his wife.

⁴And he went in unto Hagar, and she conceived: and when she saw that she had conceived, her mistress was despised in her eyes. ⁵And Sarai said unto Abram, My wrong *be* upon thee: I have given my maid into thy bosom; and when she saw that she had

GENESIS

conceived, I was despised in her eyes: the LORD judge between me and thee. ⁶But Abram said unto Sarai, Behold, thy maid *is* in thy hand; do to her as it pleaseth thee. And when Sarai dealt hardly with her, she fled from her face.

⁷And the _____ of the LORD found her by a _____ of water in the _____, by the fountain in the way to Shur. ⁸And he said, Hagar, Sarai's maid, whence camest thou? and whither wilt thou go? And she said, I flee from the face of my mistress Sarai. ⁹And the angel of the LORD said unto her, _____ to thy mistress, and _____ thyself under her hands. ¹⁰And the angel of the LORD said unto her, I will multiply thy seed exceedingly, that it shall not be numbered for multitude. ¹¹And the angel of the LORD said unto her, Behold, thou *art* with child, and shalt bear a son, and shalt call his name _____; because the LORD hath heard thy affliction. ¹²And he will be a wild man; his hand *will be* against every man, and every man's hand against him; and he shall dwell in the presence of all his brethren. ¹³And she called the name of the LORD that spake unto her, Thou God seest me: for she said, Have I also here looked after him that seeth me? ¹⁴Wherefore the well was called _____; behold, *it is* between Kadesh and Bered.

¹⁵And Hagar bare Abram a son: and Abram called his son's name, which Hagar bare, Ishmael. ¹⁶And Abram *was* fourscore and six years old, when Hagar bare Ishmael to Abram.

¹⁷:¹And when Abram was _____ years old and _____, the LORD appeared to Abram, and said unto him, I *am* the _____ God; walk before me, and be thou _____. ²And I will make my _____ between me and thee, and will multiply thee exceedingly. ³And Abram fell on his face: and God talked with him, saying, ⁴As for me, behold, my covenant *is* with thee, and thou shalt be a father of many nations. ⁵Neither shall thy name any more be called _____, but thy name shall be _____; for a father of many nations have I made thee. ⁶And I will make thee exceeding fruitful, and I will make nations of thee, and kings shall come out of thee. ⁷And I will establish my covenant between me and thee and thy _____ after thee in their generations for an _____ covenant, to be a God unto thee, and to thy seed after thee. ⁸And I will give unto thee, and to thy seed after thee, the land wherein thou art a stranger, all the land of Canaan, for an everlasting _____; and I will be their _____.

⁹And God said unto Abraham, Thou shalt keep my covenant therefore, thou, and thy seed after thee in their generations. ¹⁰This *is* my covenant, which ye shall keep, between me and you and thy seed after thee; Every man child among you shall be _____. ¹¹And ye shall circumcise the flesh of your foreskin; and it shall be a _____ of the _____ betwixt me and you. ¹²And he that is _____ _____ old shall be circumcised among you, every man child in your generations, he that is born in the house, or bought with money of any stranger, which *is* not of thy seed. ¹³He that is born in thy house, and he that is bought with thy money, must needs be circumcised: and my covenant shall be in your flesh for an everlasting covenant. ¹⁴And the uncircumcised man child whose flesh of his foreskin is not circumcised, that soul shall be cut off from his people; he hath broken my covenant.

¹⁵And God said unto Abraham, As for _____ thy wife, thou shalt not call her name Sarai, but _____ *shall* her name *be*. ¹⁶And I will _____ her, and give thee a son also of her: yea, I will bless her, and she shall be *a mother* of nations; kings of people shall be of her. ¹⁷Then Abraham fell upon his face, and _____, and said in his heart, Shall *a child* be born unto him that is an hundred years old? and shall Sarah, that is ninety

years old, bear? ¹⁸And Abraham said unto God, O that Ishmael might live before thee! ¹⁹And God said, Sarah thy wife shall bear thee a son indeed; and thou shalt call his name _____: and I will establish my covenant with _____ for an everlasting covenant, *and* with his _____ after him. ²⁰And as for Ishmael, I have heard thee: Behold, I have blessed him, and will make him fruitful, and will multiply him exceedingly; twelve princes shall he beget, and I will make him a great nation. ²¹But my covenant will I establish with _____, which Sarah shall bear unto thee at this set time in the next year. ²²And he left off talking with him, and God went up from Abraham.

²³And Abraham took Ishmael his son, and all that were born in his house, and all that were bought with his money, every male among the men of Abraham's house; and circumcised the flesh of their foreskin in the selfsame day, as God had said unto him. ²⁴And Abraham *was* ninety years old and nine, when he was circumcised in the flesh of his foreskin. ²⁵And Ishmael his son *was* thirteen years old, when he was circumcised in the flesh of his foreskin. ²⁶In the selfsame day was Abraham circumcised, and Ishmael his son. ²⁷And all the men of his house, born in the house, and bought with money of the stranger, were circumcised with him.

¹⁸:¹And the LORD appeared unto him in the plains of Mamre: and he sat in the tent door in the heat of the day; ²And he lift up his eyes and looked, and, lo, _____ men stood by him: and when he saw *them,* he ran to meet them from the tent door, and bowed himself toward the ground, ³And said, My Lord, if now I have found favour in thy sight, pass not away, I pray thee, from thy servant: ⁴Let a little water, I pray you, be fetched, and wash your feet, and rest yourselves under the tree: ⁵And I will fetch a morsel of bread, and comfort ye your hearts; after that ye shall pass on: for therefore are ye come to your servant. And they said, So do, as thou hast said. ⁶And Abraham hastened into the tent unto Sarah, and said, Make ready quickly three measures of fine meal, knead *it,* and make cakes upon the hearth. ⁷And Abraham ran unto the herd, and fetcht a calf tender and good, and gave *it* unto a young man; and he hasted to dress it. ⁸And he took butter, and milk, and the calf which he had dressed, and set *it* before them; and he stood by them under the tree, and they did eat.

⁹And they said unto him, Where *is* Sarah thy wife? And he said, Behold, in the tent. ¹⁰And he said, I will certainly return unto thee according to the time of life; and, lo, Sarah thy wife shall have a _____. And Sarah heard *it* in the tent door, which *was* behind him. ¹¹Now Abraham and Sarah *were* old *and* well stricken in age; *and* it ceased to be with Sarah after the manner of women. ¹²Therefore Sarah _____ within herself, saying, After I am waxed old shall I have pleasure, my lord being old also? ¹³And the LORD said unto Abraham, Wherefore did Sarah laugh, saying, Shall I of a surety bear a child, which am old? ¹⁴Is _____ _____ too _____ for the _____? At the time appointed I will return unto thee, according to the time of life, and Sarah shall have a son. ¹⁵Then Sarah denied, saying, I laughed not; for she was _____. And he said, Nay; but thou didst laugh.

¹⁶And the men rose up from thence, and looked toward Sodom: and Abraham went with them to bring them on the way. ¹⁷And the LORD said, Shall I _____ from Abraham that thing which I do; ¹⁸Seeing that Abraham shall surely become a great and mighty nation, and all the nations of the earth shall be blessed in him? ¹⁹For I _____ him, that he will _____ his _____ and his _____ after him, and they _____ keep the _____ of the _____, to do _____ and _____; that the LORD may

bring upon Abraham that which he hath spoken of him. [20]And the Lord said, Because the cry of Sodom and Gomorrah is great, and because their _____ is very _____; [21]I will go down now, and see whether they have done altogether according to the cry of it, which is come unto me; and if not, I will know. [22]And the men turned their faces from thence, and went toward Sodom: but Abraham stood yet before the Lord. [23]And Abraham drew near, and said, Wilt thou also destroy the righteous with the wicked? [24]Peradventure there be _____ righteous within the city: wilt thou also destroy and not spare the place for the fifty righteous that *are* therein? [25]That be far from thee to do after this manner, to slay the righteous with the wicked: and that the righteous should be as the wicked, that be far from thee: Shall not the _____ of all the earth do _____? [26]And the Lord said, If I find in Sodom fifty righteous within the city, then I will spare all the place for their sakes. [27]And Abraham answered and said, Behold now, I have taken upon me to speak unto the Lord, which *am but* dust and ashes: [28]Peradventure there shall lack five of the fifty righteous: wilt thou destroy all the city for *lack of* five? And he said, If I find there forty and five, I will _____ destroy *it*. [29]And he spake unto him yet again, and said, Peradventure there shall be forty found there. And he said, I will _____ do *it* for forty's sake. [30]And he said *unto him,* Oh let not the Lord be angry, and I will speak: Peradventure there shall thirty be found there. And he said, I will _____ do *it,* if I find thirty there. [31]And he said, Behold now, I have taken upon me to speak unto the Lord: Peradventure there shall be _____ found there. And he said, I will not destroy *it* for twenty's sake. [32]And he said, Oh let not the Lord be angry, and I will speak yet but this once: Peradventure _____ shall be found there. And he said, I will _____ destroy *it* for ten's sake. [33]And the Lord went his way, as soon as he had left communing with Abraham: and Abraham returned unto his place.

[19:1]And there came two angels to Sodom at even; and Lot _____ in the _____ of _____: and Lot seeing *them* rose up to meet them; and he bowed himself with his face toward the ground; [2]And he said, Behold now, my lords, turn in, I pray you, into your servant's house, and tarry all night, and wash your feet, and ye shall rise up early, and go on your ways. And they said, Nay; but we will abide in the street all night. [3]And he pressed upon them greatly; and they turned in unto him, and entered into his house; and he made them a feast, and did bake unleavened bread, and they did eat.

[4]But before they lay down, the men of the city, *even* the men of Sodom, compassed the house round, both old and young, all the people from every quarter: [5]And they _____ unto Lot, and said unto him, Where *are* the _____ which came in to thee this night? bring them out unto us, that we may _____ them. [6]And Lot went out at the door unto them, and shut the door after him, [7]And said, I pray you, _____, do not so _____. [8]Behold now, I have two _____ which have not known man; let me, I pray you, bring them out unto you, and _____ ye to them as *is* good in your eyes: only unto these men do nothing; for therefore came they under the shadow of my roof. [9]And they said, Stand back. And they said *again,* This one *fellow* came in to sojourn, and he will needs be a judge: now will we deal worse with thee, than with them. And they pressed sore upon the man, *even* Lot, and came near to break the door. [10]But the men put forth their hand, and pulled Lot into the house to them, and shut to the door. [11]And they _____ the men that *were* at the door of the house with _____, both small and great: so that they wearied themselves to find the door.

¹²And the men said unto Lot, Hast thou here any besides? _____ in law, and thy _____, and thy _____, and whatsoever thou hast in the city, bring *them* out of this place: ¹³For we will _____ this place, _____ the cry of them is waxen great before the face of the LORD; and the LORD hath sent us to destroy it. ¹⁴And Lot went out, and spake unto his _____ in law, which married his _____, and said, Up, get you out of this place; for the LORD will destroy this city. But he seemed as one that mocked unto his sons in law.

¹⁵And when the morning arose, then the angels hastened Lot, saying, Arise, take thy wife, and thy two daughters, which are here; lest thou be consumed in the iniquity of the city. ¹⁶And while he lingered, the men laid hold upon his hand, and upon the hand of his wife, and upon the hand of his two daughters; the LORD being _____ unto him: and they brought him forth, and set him without the city.

¹⁷And it came to pass, when they had brought them forth abroad, that he said, Escape for thy life; look _____ behind thee, neither stay thou in all the plain; escape to the mountain, lest thou be consumed. ¹⁸And Lot said unto them, Oh, not so, my Lord: ¹⁹Behold now, thy servant hath found grace in thy sight, and thou hast magnified thy mercy, which thou hast shewed unto me in saving my _____; and I cannot escape to the mountain, lest some evil take me, and I die: ²⁰Behold now, this city is near to flee unto, and it is a little one: Oh, let me escape thither, (*is* it not a little one?) and my soul shall live. ²¹And he said unto him, See, I have accepted thee concerning this thing also, that I will not overthrow this city, for the which thou hast spoken. ²²Haste thee, escape thither; for I cannot do any thing till thou be come thither. Therefore the name of the city was called Zoar.

²³The sun was risen upon the earth when Lot entered into Zoar. ²⁴Then the LORD rained upon Sodom and upon Gomorrah _____ and _____ from the LORD out of heaven; ²⁵And he overthrew those cities, and all the plain, and all the inhabitants of the cities, and that which grew upon the ground.

²⁶But his wife _____ back from behind him, and she became a pillar of _____.

²⁷And Abraham gat up early in the morning to the place where he stood before the LORD: ²⁸And he looked toward Sodom and Gomorrah, and toward all the land of the plain, and beheld, and, lo, the _____ of the country went up as the smoke of a _____.

²⁹And it came to pass, when God destroyed the cities of the plain, that God remembered Abraham, and sent Lot out of the midst of the overthrow, when he overthrew the cities in the which Lot dwelt.

³⁰And Lot went up out of Zoar, and dwelt in the mountain, and his two daughters with him; for he feared to dwell in Zoar: and he dwelt in a cave, he and his two daughters. ³¹And the firstborn said unto the younger, Our father *is* old, and *there is* not a man in the earth to come in unto us after the manner of all the earth: ³²Come, let us make our father drink _____, and we will lie with him, that we may preserve seed of our father. ³³And they made their father drink wine that night: and the firstborn went in, and lay with her father; and he perceived not when she lay down, nor when she arose. ³⁴And it came to pass on the morrow, that the firstborn said unto the younger, Behold, I lay yesternight with my father: let us make him drink wine this night also; and go thou in, *and* lie with him, that we may preserve seed of our father. ³⁵And they made their father drink wine that night also: and the younger arose, and lay with him; and he perceived not when she

lay down, nor when she arose. ³⁶Thus were both the _____ of Lot with _____ by their _____. ³⁷And the firstborn bare a son, and called his name _____: the same *is* the father of the Moabites unto this day. ³⁸And the younger, she also bare a son, and called his name _____: the same *is* the father of the children of _____ unto this day.

²⁰:¹And Abraham journeyed from thence toward the south country, and dwelled between Kadesh and Shur, and sojourned in Gerar. ²And Abraham said of Sarah his wife, She *is* my _____: and _____ king of Gerar sent, and took Sarah. ³But God came to Abimelech in a dream by night, and said to him, Behold, thou *art but* a dead man, for the woman which thou hast taken; for she *is* a man's wife. ⁴But Abimelech had not come near her: and he said, Lord, wilt thou slay also a righteous nation? ⁵Said he not unto me, She *is* my sister? and she, even she herself said, He *is* my _____: in the integrity of my heart and _____ of my hands have I done this. ⁶And God said unto him in a dream, Yea, I know that thou didst this in the integrity of thy heart; for I also withheld thee from _____ against me: therefore suffered I thee not to _____ her. ⁷Now therefore restore the man *his* wife; for he *is* a _____, and he shall _____ for thee, and thou shalt live: and if thou restore *her* not, know thou that thou shalt surely die, thou, and all that *are* thine. ⁸Therefore Abimelech rose early in the morning, and called all his servants, and told all these things in their ears: and the men were sore afraid. ⁹Then Abimelech called Abraham, and said unto him, What hast thou done unto us? and what have I offended thee, that thou hast brought on me and on my kingdom a great _____? thou hast done deeds unto me that ought not to be done. ¹⁰And Abimelech said unto Abraham, What sawest thou, that thou hast done this thing? ¹¹And Abraham said, Because I thought, Surely the fear of God *is* not in this place; and they will slay me for my wife's sake. ¹²And yet indeed *she is* my _____; she *is* the _____ of my father, but not the daughter of my _____; and she became my _____. ¹³And it came to pass, when God caused me to wander from my father's house, that I said unto her, This *is* thy kindness which thou shalt shew unto me; at every place whither we shall come, say of me, He *is* my brother. ¹⁴And Abimelech took sheep, and oxen, and menservants, and womenservants, and gave *them* unto Abraham, and restored him Sarah his wife. ¹⁵And Abimelech said, Behold, my land *is* before thee: dwell where it pleaseth thee. ¹⁶And unto Sarah he said, Behold, I have given thy brother a thousand *pieces* of silver: behold, he *is* to thee a covering of the eyes, unto all that *are* with thee, and with all *other:* thus she was reproved.

¹⁷So Abraham prayed unto God: and God _____ Abimelech, and his wife, and his maidservants; and they bare *children*. ¹⁸For the LORD had fast closed up all the wombs of the house of Abimelech, because of Sarah Abraham's wife.

²¹:¹And the LORD visited Sarah as he had said, and the LORD did unto Sarah as he had spoken. ²For Sarah _____, and bare Abraham a _____ in his old age, at the set time of which God had spoken to him. ³And Abraham called the name of his son that was born unto him, whom Sarah bare to him, _____. ⁴And Abraham circumcised his son Isaac being _____ days old, as God had commanded him. ⁵And Abraham was an hundred years old, when his son Isaac was born unto him.

⁶And Sarah said, God hath made me to laugh, *so that* all that hear will laugh with me. ⁷And she said, Who would have said unto Abraham, that Sarah should have given

children suck? for I have born *him* a son in his old age. [8]And the child grew, and was weaned: and Abraham made a great feast the *same* day that Isaac was weaned.

[9]And Sarah saw the son of Hagar the Egyptian, which she had born unto Abraham, mocking. [10]Wherefore she said unto Abraham, _____ out this bondwoman and her _____: for the son of this bondwoman shall not be _____ with my son, *even* with Isaac. [11]And the thing was very grievous in Abraham's sight because of his son.

[12]And God said unto Abraham, Let it not be grievous in thy sight because of the lad, and because of thy bondwoman; in all that Sarah hath said unto thee, hearken unto her voice; for in _____ shall thy seed be called. [13]And also of the son of the bondwoman will I make a nation, because he *is* thy seed. [14]And Abraham rose up early in the morning, and took _____, and a bottle of _____, and gave *it* unto Hagar, putting *it* on her shoulder, and the child, and sent her away: and she departed, and wandered in the wilderness of Beer-sheba. [15]And the water was spent in the bottle, and she cast the child under one of the _____. [16]And she went, and sat her down over against *him* a good way off, as it were a bowshot: for she said, Let me not see the death of the child. And she sat over against *him,* and lift up her voice, and wept. [17]And God heard the voice of the lad; and the angel of God called Hagar out of heaven, and said unto her, What aileth thee, Hagar? fear not; for God hath heard the voice of the lad where he *is.* [18]Arise, lift up the lad, and hold him in thine hand; for I will make him a great nation. [19]And God opened her eyes, and she saw a well of water; and she went, and filled the bottle with water, and gave the lad drink. [20]And God was with the lad; and he grew, and dwelt in the wilderness, and became an archer. [21]And he dwelt in the wilderness of Paran: and his mother took him a wife out of the land of Egypt.

[22]And it came to pass at that time, that Abimelech and Phichol the chief captain of his host spake unto Abraham, saying, God *is* with thee in all that thou doest: [23]Now therefore swear unto me here by God that thou wilt not deal falsely with me, nor with my son, nor with my son's son: *but* according to the kindness that I have done unto thee, thou shalt do unto me, and to the land wherein thou hast sojourned. [24]And Abraham said, I will swear. [25]And Abraham reproved Abimelech because of a _____ of water, which Abimelech's servants had violently taken away. [26]And Abimelech said, I wot not who hath done this thing: neither didst thou tell me, neither yet heard I *of it,* but to day. [27]And Abraham took sheep and oxen, and gave them unto Abimelech; and both of them made a covenant. [28]And Abraham set seven ewe lambs of the flock by themselves. [29]And Abimelech said unto Abraham, What *mean* these seven ewe lambs which thou hast set by themselves? [30]And he said, For *these* seven ewe lambs shalt thou take of my hand, that they may be a witness unto me, that I have digged this well. [31]Wherefore he called that place Beer-sheba; because there they sware both of them. [32]Thus they made a covenant at Beer-sheba: then Abimelech rose up, and Phichol the chief captain of his host, and they returned into the land of the Philistines.

[33]And *Abraham* planted a grove in Beer-sheba, and called there on the name of the LORD, the _____ God. [34]And Abraham sojourned in the Philistines' land many days.

[22:1]And it came to pass after these things, that God did tempt Abraham, and said unto him, Abraham: and he said, Behold, *here* I *am.* [2]And he said, Take now thy son, thine _____ *son* Isaac, whom thou _____, and get thee into the land of Moriah; and _____ him there for a burnt _____ upon one of the mountains which I will tell thee of.

³And Abraham rose up _____ in the morning, and saddled his ass, and took two of his young men with him, and Isaac his son, and clave the wood for the burnt offering, and _____ up, and _____ unto the _____ of which God had _____ him. ⁴Then on the third day Abraham lifted up his eyes, and saw the place afar off. ⁵And Abraham said unto his young men, Abide ye here with the ass; and I and the lad will _____ yonder and _____, and come _____ to you, ⁶And Abraham took the wood of the burnt offering, and laid *it* upon Isaac his son; and he took the fire in his hand, and a knife; and they went both of them together. ⁷And Isaac spake unto Abraham his father, and said, My father: and he said, Here *am* I, my son. And he said, Behold the fire and the wood: but where *is* the _____ for a burnt offering? ⁸And Abraham said, My son, _____ will provide _____ a _____ for a burnt offering: so they went both of them together. ⁹And they came to the place which God had told him of; and Abraham built an altar there, and laid the wood in order, and bound Isaac his son, and laid him on the altar upon the wood. ¹⁰And Abraham stretched forth his hand, and took the knife to slay his son. ¹¹And the angel of the LORD called unto him out of heaven, and said, Abraham, Abraham: and he said, Here *am* I. ¹²And he said, Lay not thine hand upon the lad, neither do thou any thing unto him: for now I _____ that thou _____ God, seeing thou hast _____ withheld thy son, thine only *son* from me. ¹³And Abraham lifted up his eyes, and looked, and behold _____ *him* a ram caught in a thicket by his horns: and Abraham went and took the ram, and offered him up for a burnt offering _____ the _____ of his son. ¹⁴And Abraham called the name of that place _____ - _____: as it is said *to* this day, In the mount of the LORD it shall be seen.

¹⁵And the angel of the LORD called unto Abraham out of heaven the second time, ¹⁶And said, By myself have I _____, saith the LORD, for because thou hast done this thing, and hast not withheld thy son, thine only *son*: ¹⁷ _____ in blessing I will _____ thee, and in multiplying I will _____ thy seed as the stars of the heaven, and as the sand which *is* upon the sea shore; and thy seed shall possess the gate of his enemies; ¹⁸And in thy seed shall all the nations of the earth be blessed; _____ thou hast _____ my voice. ¹⁹So Abraham returned unto his young men, and they rose up and went together to Beer-sheba; and Abraham dwelt at Beer-sheba.

²⁰And it came to pass after these things, that it was told Abraham, saying, Behold, Milcah, she hath also born children unto thy brother Nahor; ²¹Huz his firstborn, and Buz his brother, and Kemuel the father of Aram, ²²And Chesed, and Hazo, and Pildash, and Jidlaph, and Bethuel. ²³And Bethuel begat _____: these eight Milcah did bear to Nahor, Abraham's brother. ²⁴And his concubine, whose name *was* Reumah, she bare also Tebah, and Gaham, and Thahash, and Maachah.

²³:¹And Sarah was an hundred and seven and twenty years old: *these were* the years of the life of Sarah. ²And Sarah died in _____ - _____; the same *is* _____ in the land of Canaan: and Abraham came to mourn for Sarah, and to weep for her.

³And Abraham stood up from before his dead, and spake unto the sons of Heth, saying, ⁴I *am* a stranger and a sojourner with you: give me a possession of a buryingplace with you, that I may bury my dead out of my sight. ⁵And the children of Heth answered Abraham, saying unto him, ⁶Hear us, my lord: thou *art* a mighty prince among us: in the choice of our sepulchres bury thy dead; none of us shall withhold from thee his sepulchre, but that thou mayest bury thy dead. ⁷And Abraham stood up, and bowed himself to the people of the land, *even* to the children of Heth. ⁸And he communed with them, saying, If

it be your mind that I should bury my dead out of my sight; hear me, and intreat for me to Ephron the son of Zohar, ⁹That he may give me the cave of Machpelah, which he hath, which *is* in the end of his field; for as much money as it is worth he shall give it me for a possession of a buryingplace amongst you. ¹⁰And Ephron dwelt among the children of Heth: and Ephron the Hittite answered Abraham in the audience of the children of Heth, *even* of all that went in at the gate of his city, saying, ¹¹Nay, my lord, hear me: the field give I thee, and the cave that *is* therein, I give it thee; in the presence of the sons of my people give I it thee: bury thy dead. ¹²And Abraham bowed down himself before the people of the land. ¹³And he spake unto Ephron in the audience of the people of the land, saying, But if thou *wilt give it,* I pray thee, hear me: I will give thee money for the field; take *it* of me, and I will bury my dead there. ¹⁴And Ephron answered Abraham, saying unto him, ¹⁵My lord, hearken unto me: the land *is worth* four hundred shekels of silver; what *is* that betwixt me and thee? bury therefore thy dead. ¹⁶And Abraham hearkened unto Ephron; and Abraham weighed to Ephron the silver, which he had named in the audience of the sons of Heth, four hundred shekels of silver, current *money* with the merchant.

¹⁷And the field of Ephron, which *was* in Machpelah, which *was* before Mamre, the field, and the cave which *was* therein, and all the trees that *were* in the field, that *were* in all the borders round about, were made sure ¹⁸Unto Abraham for a possession in the presence of the children of Heth, before all that went in at the gate of his city. ¹⁹And after this, Abraham buried Sarah his wife in the cave of the field of Machpelah before Mamre: the same *is* Hebron in the land of Canaan. ²⁰And the field, and the cave that *is* therein, were made sure unto Abraham for a possession of a buryingplace by the sons of Heth.

²⁴:¹And Abraham was old, *and* well stricken in age: and the Lord had blessed Abraham in all things. ²And Abraham said unto his eldest servant of his house, that ruled over all that he had, Put, I pray thee, thy hand under my thigh: ³And I will make thee swear by the Lord, the God of heaven, and the God of the earth, that thou shalt _____ take a _____ unto my son of the daughters of the _____, among whom I dwell: ⁴But thou shalt go unto _____ _____, and to _____ _____, and take a wife unto my son Isaac. ⁵And the servant said unto him, Peradventure the woman will not be willing to follow me unto this land: must I needs bring thy son again unto the land from whence thou camest? ⁶And Abraham said unto him, _____ thou that thou bring _____ my son _____ again.

⁷The Lord God of heaven, which took me _____ my father's house, and from the land of my kindred, and which spake unto me, and that sware unto me, saying, Unto thy seed will I give this land; he shall send his angel before thee, and thou shalt take a wife unto my son from thence. ⁸And if the woman will not be willing to follow thee, then thou shalt be clear from this my oath: only bring not my son thither again. ⁹And the servant put his hand under the thigh of Abraham his master, and sware to him concerning that matter.

¹⁰And the servant took ten camels of the camels of his master, and departed; for all the goods of his master *were* in his hand: and he arose, and went to Mesopotamia, unto the city of Nahor. ¹¹And he made his camels to kneel down without the city by a well of water at the time of the evening, *even* the time that women go out to draw *water.* ¹²And he said, O Lord God of my master Abraham, I _____ thee, send me good speed this day, and shew kindness unto my master Abraham. ¹³Behold, I stand *here* by the _____ of water; and the daughters of the men of the city come out to draw water:

GENESIS

¹⁴And let it come to pass, that the damsel to whom I shall say, Let down thy pitcher, I pray thee, that I may drink; and she shall say, Drink, and I will give thy camels drink also: *let the same be* she *that* thou hast _____ for thy servant Isaac; and thereby shall I know that thou hast shewed kindness unto my master.

¹⁵And it came to pass, before he had done speaking, that, behold, Rebekah came out, who was born to Bethuel, son of Milcah, the wife of Nahor, Abraham's brother, with her pitcher upon her shoulder. ¹⁶And the damsel *was* very fair to look upon, a _____, neither had any man known her: and she went down to the well, and filled her pitcher, and came up. ¹⁷And the servant _____ to meet her, and said, Let me, I pray thee, drink a little water of thy pitcher. ¹⁸And she said, Drink, my lord: and she _____, and let down her pitcher upon her hand, and gave him drink. ¹⁹And when she had done giving him drink, she said, I will draw *water* for thy camels also, until they have done drinking. ²⁰And she _____, and emptied her pitcher into the trough, and _____ again unto the well to draw *water,* and drew for all his camels. ²¹And the man wondering at her held his peace, to wit whether the LORD had made his journey prosperous or not. ²²And it came to pass, as the camels had done drinking, that the man took a golden earring of half a shekel weight, and two bracelets for her hands of ten *shekels* weight of gold; ²³And said, Whose daughter *art* thou? tell me, I pray thee: is there room *in* thy father's house for us to lodge in? ²⁴And she said unto him, I *am* the daughter of Bethuel the son of Milcah, which she bare unto Nahor. ²⁵She said moreover unto him, We have both straw and provender enough, and room to lodge in. ²⁶And the man bowed down his head, and _____ the LORD. ²⁷And he said, Blessed *be* the LORD God of my master Abraham, who hath not left destitute my master of his mercy and his truth: I *being* in the _____, the LORD _____ me to the house of my master's brethren. ²⁸And the damsel ran, and told *them of* her mother's house these things.

²⁹And Rebekah had a brother, and his name *was* _____: and Laban ran out unto the man, unto the well. ³⁰And it came to pass, when he saw the earring and bracelets upon his sister's hands, and when he heard the words of Rebekah his sister, saying, Thus spake the man unto me; that he came unto the man; and, behold, he stood by the camels at the well. ³¹And he said, Come in, thou blessed of the LORD; wherefore standest thou without? for I have prepared the house, and room for the camels.

³²And the man came into the house: and he ungirded his camels, and gave straw and provender for the camels, and water to wash his feet, and the men's feet that *were* with him. ³³And there was set *meat* before him to eat: but he said, I will not eat, until I have told mine errand. And he said, Speak on. ³⁴And he said, I *am* Abraham's servant. ³⁵And the LORD hath blessed my master greatly; and he is become great: and he hath given him flocks, and herds, and silver, and gold, and menservants, and maidservants, and camels, and asses. ³⁶And Sarah my master's wife bare a son to my master when she was old: and unto him hath he given all that he hath. ³⁷And my master made me swear, saying, Thou shalt not take a wife to my son of the daughters of the Canaanites, in whose land I dwell: ³⁸But thou shalt go unto my father's house, and to my kindred, and take a wife unto my son. ³⁹And I said unto my master, Peradventure the woman will not follow me. ⁴⁰And he said unto me, The LORD, before whom I walk, will send his angel with thee, and prosper thy way; and thou shalt take a wife for my son of my kindred, and of my father's house: ⁴¹Then shalt thou be clear from *this* my oath, when thou comest to my kindred; and if they give not thee *one,* thou shalt be clear from my oath. ⁴²And I came this day unto the

well, and said, O LORD God of my master Abraham, if now thou do prosper my way which I go; ⁴³Behold, I stand by the well of water; and it shall come to pass, that when the virgin cometh forth to draw *water,* and I say to her, Give me, I pray thee, a little water of thy pitcher to drink; ⁴⁴And she say to me, Both drink thou, and I will also draw for thy camels: *let* the same *be* the woman whom the LORD hath appointed out for my master's son. ⁴⁵And before I had done speaking in mine heart, behold, Rebekah came forth with her pitcher on her shoulder; and she went down unto the well, and drew *water:* and I said unto her, Let me drink, I pray thee. ⁴⁶And she made haste, and let down her pitcher from her *shoulder,* and said, Drink, and I will give thy camels drink also: so I drank, and she made the camels drink also. ⁴⁷And I asked her, and said, Whose daughter *art* thou? And she said, The daughter of Bethuel, Nahor's son, whom Milcah bare unto him: and I put the earring upon her face, and the bracelets upon her hands. ⁴⁸And I bowed down my head, and worshipped the LORD, and blessed the LORD God of my master Abraham, which had led me in the right way to take my master's brother's daughter unto his son. ⁴⁹And now if ye will deal kindly and truly with my master, tell me: and if not, tell me; that I may turn to the right hand, or to the left. ⁵⁰Then Laban and Bethuel answered and said, The thing proceedeth from the LORD: we cannot speak unto thee bad or good. ⁵¹Behold, Rebekah *is* before thee, take *her,* and go, and let her be thy master's son's wife, as the LORD hath spoken. ⁵²And it came to pass, that, when Abraham's servant heard their words, he worshipped the LORD, *bowing himself* to the earth. ⁵³And the servant brought forth jewels of silver, and jewels of gold, and raiment, and gave *them* to Rebekah: he gave also to her brother and to her mother precious things. ⁵⁴And they did eat and drink, he and the men that *were* with him, and tarried all night; and they rose up in the morning, and he said, Send me away unto my master. ⁵⁵And her brother and her mother said, Let the damsel abide with us *a few* days, at the least ten; after that she shall go. ⁵⁶And he said unto them, Hinder me not, seeing the LORD hath prospered my way; send me away that I may go to my master. ⁵⁷And they said, We will call the damsel, and enquire at her mouth. ⁵⁸And they called Rebekah, and said unto her, Wilt thou go with this man? And she said, I will go. ⁵⁹And they sent away Rebekah their sister, and her nurse, and Abraham's servant, and his men. ⁶⁰And they blessed Rebekah, and said unto her, Thou *art* our sister, be thou *the mother* of thousands of millions, and let thy seed possess the gate of those which hate them.

⁶¹And Rebekah arose, and her damsels, and they rode upon the camels, and followed the man: and the servant took Rebekah, and went his way. ⁶²And Isaac came from the way of the _____ _____-_____; for he dwelt in the south country. ⁶³And Isaac went out to _____ in the field at the eventide: and he lifted up his eyes, and saw, and, behold, the camels *were* coming. ⁶⁴And Rebekah lifted up her eyes, and when she saw Isaac, she lighted off the camel. ⁶⁵For she *had* said unto the servant, What man *is* this that walketh in the field to meet us? And the servant *had* said, It *is* my master: therefore she took a vail, and covered herself. ⁶⁶And the servant told Isaac all things that he had done. ⁶⁷And Isaac brought her into his mother Sarah's tent, and took Rebekah, and she became his wife; and he loved her: and Isaac was comforted after his mother's *death.*

²⁵:¹Then again Abraham took a _____, and her name *was* _____. ²And she bare him Zimran, and Jokshan, and _____, and _____, and Ishbak, and Shuah. ³And Jokshan begat Sheba, and Dedan. And the sons of Dedan were Asshurim, and Letushim,

and Leummim. ⁴And the sons of Midian; Ephah, and Epher, and Hanoch, and Abidah, and Eldaah. All these *were* the children of Keturah.

⁵And Abraham gave _____ that he had unto _____. ⁶But unto the sons of the concubines, which Abraham had, Abraham gave gifts, and sent them away from Isaac his son, while he yet lived, _____, unto the _____ country. ⁷And these *are* the days of the years of Abraham's life which he lived, an hundred threescore and fifteen years. ⁸Then Abraham gave up the ghost, and died in a good old age, an old man, and full *of years;* and was gathered to his people. ⁹And his sons Isaac and Ishmael buried him in the cave of Machpelah, in the field of Ephron the son of Zohar the Hittite, which *is* before Mamre; ¹⁰The field which Abraham purchased of the sons of Heth: there was Abraham buried, and Sarah his wife.

¹¹And it came to pass after the death of Abraham, that God blessed his son Isaac; and Isaac _____ by the _____ Lahai-roi.

¹²Now these *are* the generations of Ishmael, Abraham's son, whom Hagar the Egyptian, Sarah's handmaid, bare unto Abraham: ¹³And these *are* the names of the sons of Ishmael, by their names, according to their generations: the firstborn of Ishmael, Nebajoth; and Kedar, and Adbeel, and Mibsam, ¹⁴And Mishma, and Dumah, and Massa, ¹⁵Hadar, and Tema, Jetur, Naphish, and Kedemah: ¹⁶These *are* the sons of Ishmael, and these *are* their names, by their towns, and by their castles; twelve princes according to their nations. ¹⁷And these *are* the years of the life of Ishmael, an hundred and thirty and seven years: and he gave up the ghost and died; and was gathered unto his people. ¹⁸And they dwelt from Havilah unto Shur, that *is* before Egypt, as thou goest toward Assyria: *and* he died in the presence of all his brethren.

¹⁹And these *are* the generations of Isaac, Abraham's son: Abraham begat Isaac: ²⁰And Isaac was forty years old when he took Rebekah to wife, the daughter of Bethuel the Syrian of Padan-aram, the sister to Laban the Syrian. ²¹And Isaac intreated the LORD for his wife, because she *was* _____: and the LORD was intreated of him, and Rebekah his wife conceived. ²²And the _____ struggled together within her; and she said, If *it be* so, why *am* I thus? And she went to enquire of the LORD. ²³And the LORD said unto her, Two nations *are* in thy womb, and two manner of people shall be separated from thy bowels; and *the one* people shall be stronger than *the other* people; and the elder shall serve the younger.

²⁴And when her days to be delivered were fulfilled, behold, *there were* _____ in her womb. ²⁵And the first came out red, all over like an hairy garment; and they called his name _____. ²⁶And after that came his brother out, and his hand took hold on Esau's heel; and his name was called _____: and Isaac *was* threescore years old when she bare them. ²⁷And the boys grew: and Esau was a cunning hunter, a man of the field; and Jacob *was* a plain man, dwelling in tents. ²⁸And Isaac loved _____, because he did eat of *his* venison: but Rebekah loved _____.

²⁹And Jacob sod pottage: and Esau came from the field, and he *was* faint: ³⁰And Esau said to Jacob, Feed me, I pray thee, with that same red *pottage;* for I *am* faint: therefore was his name called Edom. ³¹And Jacob said, _____ me this day thy _____. ³²And Esau said, Behold, I *am* at the point to die: and what profit shall this birthright do to me? ³³And Jacob said, Swear to me this day; and he sware unto him: and he _____ his _____ unto Jacob. ³⁴Then Jacob gave Esau bread and pottage of lentiles; and he did eat and drink, and rose up, and went his way: thus Esau _____ *his* _____.

GENESIS

26:1And there was a famine in the land, beside the first famine that was in the days of Abraham. And Isaac went unto Abimelech king of the Philistines unto Gerar. 2And the LORD appeared unto him, and said, Go not down into Egypt; dwell in the land which I shall tell thee of: 3Sojourn in this land, and I will be with thee, and will bless thee; for unto thee, and unto thy seed, I will give all these countries, and I will perform the oath which I sware unto Abraham thy father; 4And I will make thy seed to multiply as the stars of heaven, and will give unto thy seed all these countries; and in thy seed shall all the nations of the earth be blessed; 5Because that Abraham _____my voice, and _____my _____, my _____, my _____, and my _____.

6And Isaac dwelt in Gerar: 7And the men of the place asked *him* of his wife; and he said, She *is* my _____: for he feared to say, *She is* my wife; lest, *said he,* the men of the place should kill me for Rebekah; because she *was* _____to look upon. 8And it came to pass, when he had been there a long time, that Abimelech king of the Philistines looked out at a window, and saw, and, behold, Isaac *was* sporting with Rebekah his wife. 9And Abimelech called Isaac, and said, Behold, of a surety she *is* thy wife: and how saidst thou, She *is* my sister? And Isaac said unto him, Because I said, Lest I die for her. 10And Abimelech said, What *is* this thou hast done unto us? one of the people might lightly have lien with thy wife, and thou shouldest have brought guiltiness upon us. 11And Abimelech charged all *his* people, saying, He that toucheth this man or his wife shall surely be put to death. 12Then Isaac sowed in that land, and received in the same year an hundredfold: and the LORD blessed him. 13And the man waxed great, and went forward, and grew until he became very great: 14For he had possession of flocks, and possession of herds, and great store of servants: and the Philistines _____him. 15For all the wells which his father's servants had digged in the days of Abraham his father, the _____had _____them, and _____them with _____. 16And Abimelech said unto Isaac, Go from us; for thou art much mightier than we.

17And Isaac departed thence, and pitched his tent in the valley of Gerar, and dwelt there. 18And Isaac _____again the _____of water, which they had digged in the days of Abraham his _____; for the philistines had stopped them after the death of Abraham: and he called their names after the names by which his _____had called them. 19And Isaac's servants digged in the _____, and found there a well of _____water. 20And the herdmen of Gerar did strive with Isaac's herdmen, saying, The water *is* ours: and he called the name of the well Esek; because they strove with him. 21And they digged another well, and strove for that also: and he called the name of it Sitnah. 22And he removed from thence, and digged another well; and for that they strove not: and he called the name of it _____; and he said, For now the LORD hath made room for us, and we shall be fruitful in the land. 23And he went up from thence to Beersheba. 24And the LORD appeared unto him the same night, and said, I *am* the God of Abraham thy father: fear not, for I *am* with thee, and will bless thee, and multiply thy seed for my servant Abraham's sake. 25And he builded an _____there, and called upon the name of the LORD and pitched his tent there: and there Isaac's servants digged a _____.

26Then Abimelech went to him from Gerar, and Ahuzzath one of his friends, and Phichol the chief captain of his army. 27And Isaac said unto them, Wherefore come ye to me, seeing ye hate me, and have sent me away from you? 28And they said, We saw certainly that the LORD was with thee: and we said, Let there be now an oath betwixt us, *even* betwixt us and thee, and let us make a covenant with thee; ²⁹That thou wilt do us no hurt, as we have not touched thee, and as we have done unto thee nothing but good, and have sent thee away in peace: thou *art* now the blessed of the LORD. ³⁰And he made them a feast, and they did eat and drink. ³¹And they rose up betimes in the morning, and sware one to another: and Isaac sent them away, and they departed from him in peace. ³²And it came to pass the same day, that Isaac's servants came, and told him concerning the well which they had digged, and said unto him, We have found water. ³³And he called it Shebah: therefore the name of the city *is* Beer-sheba unto this day.

³⁴And Esau was forty years old when he took to wife Judith the daughter of Beeri the Hittite, and Bashemath the daughter of Elon the Hittite: ³⁵Which were a _____ of _____ unto Isaac and to Rebekah.

²⁷:¹And it came to pass, that when Isaac was old, and his eyes were dim, so that he could not see, he called Esau his eldest son, and said unto him, My son: and he said unto him, Behold, *here am* I. ²And he said, Behold now, I am old, I know not the day of my death: ³Now therefore take, I pray thee, thy weapons, thy quiver and thy bow, and go out to the field, and take me *some* _____; ⁴And make me savoury meat, such as I love, and bring *it* to me, that I may eat; that my soul may _____ thee before I die. ⁵And Rebekah heard when Isaac spake to Esau his son. And Esau went to the field to hunt *for* venison, *and* to bring *it.*

⁶And Rebekah spake unto Jacob her son, saying, Behold, I heard thy father speak unto Esau thy brother, saying, ⁷Bring me venison, and make me savoury meat, that I may eat, and bless thee before the LORD before my death. ⁸Now therefore, my son, obey my voice according to that which I command thee. ⁹Go now to the flock, and fetch me from thence two good kids of the goats; and I will make them savoury meat for thy father, such as he loveth: ¹⁰And thou shalt bring *it* to thy father, that he may eat, and that he may bless thee before his death. ¹¹And Jacob said to Rebekah his mother, Behold, Esau my brother *is* a hairy man, and I *am* a smooth man: ¹²My father peradventure will feel me, and I shall seem to him as a deceiver; and I shall bring a curse upon me, and not a blessing. ¹³And his mother said unto him, Upon me *be* thy curse, my son: only obey my voice, and go fetch me *them.* ¹⁴And he went, and fetched, and brought *them* to his mother: and his mother made savoury meat, such as his father loved. ¹⁵And Rebekah took goodly raiment of her eldest son Esau, which *were* with her in the house, and put them upon Jacob her younger son: ¹⁶And she put the skins of the kids of the goats upon his hands, and upon the smooth of his neck: ¹⁷And she gave the savoury meat and the bread, which she had prepared, into the hand of her son Jacob.

¹⁸And he came unto his father, and said, My father: and he said, Here *am* I; who *art* thou, my son? ¹⁹And Jacob said unto his father, I *am* _____ thy firstborn; I have done according as thou badest me: arise, I pray thee, sit and eat of my venison, that thy soul may bless me. ²⁰And Isaac said unto his son, How *is it* that thou hast found *it* so quickly, my son? And he said, Because the _____ thy _____ brought *it* to me. ²¹And Isaac said unto Jacob, Come near, I pray thee, that I may feel thee, my son, whether thou *be* my very son Esau or not. ²²And Jacob went near unto Isaac his father; and he felt him, and said, The _____ *is* _____ voice, but the _____ *are* the hands of _____. ²³And he discerned him not, because his hands were hairy, as his brother Esau's hands: so he blessed him. ²⁴And he said, *Art* thou my very son _____? And he said, I _____. ²⁵And he said, Bring *it* near to me, and I will eat of my son's venison, that my soul may

bless thee. And he brought *it* near to him, and he did eat: and he brought him wine, and he drank. ²⁶And his father Isaac said unto him, Come near now, and kiss me, my son. ²⁷And he came near, and kissed him: and he smelled the smell of his raiment, and blessed him, and said, See, the smell of my son *is* as the smell of a field which the LORD hath blessed: ²⁸Therefore God give thee of the dew of heaven, and the fatness of the earth, and plenty of corn and wine: ²⁹Let people serve thee, and nations bow down to thee: be lord over thy brethren, and let thy mother's sons bow down to thee: _____ *be* every one that curseth thee, and _____ *be* he that blesseth thee.

³⁰And it came to pass, as soon as Isaac had made an end of blessing Jacob, and Jacob was yet scarce gone out from the presence of Isaac his father, that Esau his brother came in from his hunting. ³¹And he also had made savoury meat, and brought it unto his father, and said unto his father, Let my father arise, and eat of his son's venison, that thy soul may bless me. ³²And Isaac his father said unto him, Who *art* thou? And he said, I *am* thy son, thy firstborn Esau. ³³And Isaac trembled very exceedingly, and said, Who? where *is* he that hath taken venison, and brought *it* me, and I have eaten of all before thou camest, and have blessed him? yea, *and* he shall be blessed. ³⁴And when Esau heard the words of his father, he cried with a great and exceeding bitter cry, and said unto his father, Bless me, *even* me also, O my father. ³⁵And he said, Thy brother came with _____, and hath taken away thy _____. ³⁶And he said, Is not he rightly named Jacob? for he hath supplanted me these two times: he took away my _____; and, behold, now he hath taken away my _____. And he said, Hast thou not reserved a blessing for me? ³⁷And Isaac answered and said unto Esau, Behold, I have made him thy lord, and all his brethren have I given to him for servants; and with corn and wine have I sustained him: and what shall I do now unto thee, my son? ³⁸And Esau said unto his father, Hast thou but one blessing, my father? bless me, *even* me also, O my father. And Esau lifted up his voice, and wept. ³⁹And Isaac his father answered and said unto him, Behold, thy dwelling shall be the fatness of the earth, and of the dew of heaven from above; ⁴⁰And by thy sword shalt thou live, and shalt serve thy brother; and it shall come to pass when thou shalt have the dominion, that thou shalt break his yoke from off thy neck.

⁴¹And Esau _____ Jacob because of the blessing wherewith his father blessed him: and Esau said in his heart, The days of mourning for my father are at hand; then will I slay my brother Jacob. ⁴²And these words of Esau her elder son were told to Rebekah: and she sent and called Jacob her younger son, and said unto him, Behold, thy brother Esau, as touching thee, doth comfort himself, *purposing* to kill thee. ⁴³Now therefore, my son, obey my voice; and arise, flee thou to Laban my brother to Haran; ⁴⁴And tarry with him a few days, until thy brother's fury turn away; ⁴⁵Until thy brother's anger turn away from thee, and he forget *that* which thou hast done to him: then I will send, and fetch thee from thence: why should I be deprived also of you both in one day? ⁴⁶And Rebekah said to Isaac, I am weary of my life because of the daughters of Heth: if Jacob take a wife of the daughters of Heth, such as these *which are* of the daughters of the land, what good shall my life do me?

²⁸:¹And Isaac called Jacob, and _____ him, and charged him, and said unto him, Thou shalt not take a wife of the daughters of Canaan. ²Arise, go to Padan-aram, to the house of Bethuel thy mother's father; and take thee a wife from thence of the daughters of Laban thy mother's brother. ³And God Almighty bless thee, and make thee fruitful, and multiply thee, that thou mayest be a multitude of people; ⁴And give thee the blessing of

Abraham, to thee, and to thy seed with thee; that thou mayest inherit the land wherein thou art a stranger, which God gave unto Abraham. ⁵And Isaac sent away Jacob: and he went to Padan-aram unto Laban, son of Bethuel the Syrian, the brother of Rebekah, Jacob's and Esau's mother.

⁶When Esau saw that Isaac had _____ Jacob, and sent him away to Padan-aram, to take him a wife from thence; and that as he _____ him he gave him a charge, saying, Thou shalt not take a wife of the daughters of Canaan; ⁷And that Jacob obeyed his father and his mother, and was gone to Padan-aram; ⁸And Esau seeing that the daughters of Canaan pleased not Isaac his father; ⁹Then went Esau unto Ishmael, and took unto the wives which he had Mahalath the daughter of Ishmael Abraham's son, the sister of Nebajoth, to be his wife.

¹⁰And Jacob went out from Beer-sheba, and went toward Haran. ¹¹And he lighted upon a certain place, and tarried there all night, because the sun was set; and he took of the stones of that place, and *put* them for his pillows, and lay down in that place to sleep. ¹²And he dreamed, and behold a _____ set up on the earth, and the top of it reached to heaven: and behold the angels of God ascending and descending on it. ¹³And, behold, the LORD stood above it, and said, I *am* the LORD God of Abraham thy father, and the God of Isaac: the land whereon thou liest, to thee will I give it, and to thy seed; ¹⁴And thy seed shall be as the dust of the earth, and thou shalt spread abroad to the west, and to the east, and to the north, and to the south: and in thee and in thy seed shall all the families of the earth be blessed. ¹⁵And, behold, I *am* _____ thee, and will _____ thee in all *places* whither thou goest, and will bring thee again into this land; for I will not leave thee, until I have done *that* which I have spoken to thee of.

¹⁶And Jacob awaked out of his sleep, and he said, Surely the LORD is in this place; and I knew *it* not. ¹⁷And he was afraid, and said, How dreadful *is* this place! this is none other but the _____ of God, and this *is* the gate of heaven. ¹⁸And Jacob rose up early in the morning, and took the stone that he had put *for* his pillows, and set it up *for* a pillar, and poured oil upon the top of it. ¹⁹And he called the name of that place _____: but the name of that city *was called* Luz at the first. ²⁰And Jacob vowed a vow, saying, If God will be with me, and will keep me in this way that I go, and will give me bread to eat, and raiment to put on, ²¹So that I come again to my father's house in peace; then shall the LORD be my God: ²²And this stone, which I have set *for* a pillar, shall be God's house: and of all that thou shalt give me I will surely give the tenth unto thee.

²⁹:¹Then Jacob went on his journey, and came into the land of the people of the east. ²And he looked, and behold a _____ in the field, and, lo, there *were* three flocks of sheep lying by it; for out of that well they watered the flocks: and a great stone *was* upon the well's mouth. ³And thither were all the flocks gathered: and they rolled the stone from the well's mouth, and watered the sheep, and put the stone again upon the well's mouth in his place. ⁴And Jacob said unto them, My brethren, whence *be* ye? And they said, Of Haran *are* we. ⁵And he said unto them, Know ye Laban the son of Nahor? And they said, We know *him*. ⁶And he said unto them, *Is* he well? And they said, *He is* well: and, behold, Rachel his daughter cometh with the sheep. ⁷And he said, Lo, *it is* yet high day, neither *is it* time that the cattle should be gathered together: water ye the sheep, and go *and* feed *them*. ⁸And they said, We cannot, until all the flocks be gathered together, and *till* they roll the stone from the well's mouth; then we water the sheep.

⁹And while he yet spake with them, Rachel came with her father's sheep: for she kept them. ¹⁰And it came to pass, when Jacob saw Rachel the daughter of Laban his mother's brother, and the sheep of Laban his mother's brother, that Jacob went near, and rolled the stone from the well's mouth, and watered the flock of Laban his mother's brother. ¹¹And Jacob kissed Rachel, and lifted up his voice, and wept. ¹²And Jacob told Rachel that he *was* her father's brother, and that he *was* Rebekah's son: and she ran and told her father. ¹³And it came to pass, when Laban heard the tidings of Jacob his sister's son, that he ran to meet him, and embraced him, and kissed him, and brought him to his house. And he told Laban all these things. ¹⁴And Laban said to him, Surely thou *art* my bone and my flesh. And he abode with him the space of a month.

¹⁵And Laban said unto Jacob, Because thou *art* my brother, shouldest thou therefore serve me for nought? tell me, what *shall* thy wages *be?* ¹⁶And Laban had two daughters: the name of the elder *was* _____, and the name of the younger *was* _____. ¹⁷Leah *was* tender eyed; but Rachel was _____ and well favoured. ¹⁸And Jacob loved Rachel; and said, I will serve thee _____ years for _____ thy younger daughter. ¹⁹And Laban said, *It is* better that I give her to thee, than that I should give her to another man: abide with me. ²⁰And Jacob served seven years for Rachel; and they seemed unto him *but* a few _____, for the love he had to her.

²¹And Jacob said unto Laban, Give *me* my wife, for my days are fulfilled, that I may go in unto her. ²²And Laban gathered together all the men of the place, and made a feast. ²³And it came to pass in the evening, that he took _____ his daughter, and brought her to him; and he went in unto her. ²⁴And Laban gave unto his daughter Leah Zilpah his maid *for* an handmaid. ²⁵And it came to pass, that in the morning, behold, it *was* Leah: and he said to Laban, What *is* this thou hast done unto me? did not I serve with thee for _____? wherefore then hast thou beguiled me? ²⁶And Laban said, It must not be so done in our country, to give the younger before the firstborn. ²⁷Fulfil her _____, and we will give thee this also for the service which thou shalt serve with me yet _____ other years. ²⁸And Jacob did so, and fulfilled her week: and he gave him _____ his daughter to wife also. ²⁹And Laban gave to Rachel his daughter Bilhah his handmaid to be her maid. ³⁰And he went in also unto Rachel, and he _____ also Rachel more than Leah, and served with him yet _____ other years.

³¹And when the LORD saw that Leah *was* _____, he opened her _____: but Rachel *was* _____. ³²And Leah conceived, and bare a son, and she called his name _____: for she said, Surely the LORD hath looked upon my affliction; now therefore my husband will love me. ³³And she conceived again, and bare a son; and said, Because the LORD hath heard that I *was* hated, he hath therefore given me this *son* also: and she called his name _____. ³⁴And she conceived again, and bare a son; and said, Now this time will my husband be joined unto me, because I have born him three sons: therefore was his name called _____. ³⁵And she conceived again, and bare a son: and she said, Now will I praise the LORD: therefore she called his name _____; and left bearing.

³⁰:¹And when Rachel saw that she bare Jacob no children, Rachel _____ her sister; and said unto Jacob, Give me children, or else I die. ²And Jacob's anger was kindled against Rachel: and he said, *Am* I in God's stead, who hath withheld from thee the fruit of the womb? ³And she said, Behold my maid _____, go in unto her; and she shall bear upon my knees that I may also have children by her. ⁴And she gave him Bilhah her handmaid to wife: and Jacob went in unto her. ⁵And Bilhah conceived, and bare Jacob a

son. ⁶And Rachel said, God hath judged me, and hath also heard my voice, and hath given me a son: therefore called she his name _____. ⁷And Bilhah Rachel's maid conceived again, and bare Jacob a second son. ⁸And Rachel said, With great wrestlings have I wrestled with my sister, and I have prevailed: and she called his name _____. ⁹When Leah saw that she had left bearing, she took _____ her maid, and gave her Jacob to wife. ¹⁰And Zilpah Leah's maid bare Jacob a son. ¹¹And Leah said, A troop cometh: and she called his name _____. ¹²And Zilpah Leah's maid bare Jacob a second son. ¹³And Leah said, Happy am I, for the daughters will call me blessed: and she called his name _____.

¹⁴And Reuben went in the days of wheat harvest, and found mandrakes in the field, and brought them unto his mother Leah. Then Rachel said to Leah, Give me, I pray thee, of thy son's mandrakes. ¹⁵And she said unto her, *Is it* a small matter that thou hast taken my husband? and wouldest thou take away my son's mandrakes also? And Rachel said, Therefore he shall lie with thee to night for thy son's mandrakes. ¹⁶And Jacob came out of the field in the evening, and Leah went out to meet him, and said, Thou must come in unto me; for surely I have hired thee with my son's mandrakes. And he lay with her that night. ¹⁷And God hearkened unto Leah, and she conceived, and bare Jacob the fifth son. ¹⁸And Leah said, God hath given me my hire, because I have given my maiden to my husband: and she called his name _____. ¹⁹And Leah conceived again, and bare Jacob the sixth son. ²⁰And Leah said, God hath endued me *with* a good dowry; now will my husband dwell with me, because I have born him six sons: and she called his name _____. ²¹And afterwards she bare a daughter, and called her name _____.

²²And God remembered Rachel, and _____ hearkened to her, and _____ her womb. ²³And she conceived, and bare a son; and said, God hath taken away my reproach: ²⁴And she called his name _____; and said, The L ORD shall add to me another son.

²⁵And it came to pass, when Rachel had born Joseph, that Jacob said unto Laban, Send me away, that I may go unto mine own place, and to my country. ²⁶Give *me* my wives and my children, for whom I have served thee, and let me go: for thou knowest my service which I have done thee. ²⁷And Laban said unto him, I pray thee, if I have found favour in thine eyes, *tarry: for* I have learned by experience that the L ORD hath blessed me for thy sake. ²⁸And he said, Appoint me thy wages, and I will give *it.* ²⁹And he said unto him, Thou knowest how I have served thee, and how thy cattle was with me. ³⁰For *it was* little which thou hadst before I *came,* and it is *now* increased unto a multitude; and the L ORD hath blessed thee since my coming: and now when shall I provide for mine own house also? ³¹And he said, What shall I give thee? And Jacob said, Thou shalt not give me any thing: if thou wilt do this thing for me, I will again feed *and* keep thy flock: ³²I will pass through all thy flock to day, removing from thence all the _____ and _____ cattle, and all the _____ cattle among the _____, and the _____ and _____ among the _____: and *of such* shall be my hire. ³³So shall my righteousness answer for me in time to come, when it shall come for my hire before thy face: every one that *is* not speckled and spotted among the goats, and brown among the sheep, that shall be counted stolen with me. ³⁴And Laban said, Behold, I would it might be according to thy word. ³⁵And he removed that day the he goats that were ringstraked and spotted, and all the she goats that were speckled and spotted, *and* every one that had *some* white in it, and all the brown among the sheep, and gave *them* into the hand of his sons. ³⁶And he set three days' journey betwixt himself and Jacob: and Jacob fed the rest of Laban's flocks.

³⁷And Jacob took him rods of green poplar, and of the hazel and chesnut tree; and pilled white strakes in them, and made the white appear which *was* in the rods. ³⁸And he set the rods which he had pilled before the flocks in the gutters in the watering troughs when the flocks came to drink, that they should conceive when they came to drink. ³⁹And the flocks conceived before the rods, and brought forth cattle ringstraked, speckled, and spotted. ⁴⁰And Jacob did separate the lambs, and set the faces of the flocks toward the ringstraked, and all the brown in the flock of Laban; and he put his own flocks by themselves, and put them not unto Laban's cattle. ⁴¹And it came to pass, whensoever the stronger cattle did conceive, that Jacob laid the rods before the eyes of the cattle in the gutters, that they might conceive among the rods. ⁴²But when the cattle were feeble, he put *them* not in: so the feebler were Laban's, and the stronger Jacob's. ⁴³And the man increased exceedingly, and had much cattle, and maidservants, and menservants, and camels, and asses.

^{31:1}And he heard the words of Laban's sons, saying, Jacob hath taken away all that *was* our father's; and of *that* which *was* our father's hath he gotten all this glory. ²And Jacob beheld the _____ of Laban, and, behold, it *was* not toward him as before. ³And the LORD said unto Jacob, Return unto the land of thy fathers, and to thy kindred; and I will be with thee. ⁴And Jacob sent and called Rachel and Leah to the field unto his flock, ⁵And said unto them, I see your father's _____, that it *is* not toward me as before; but the God of my father hath been with me. ⁶And ye know that with all my power I have served your father. ⁷And your father hath deceived me, and changed my wages _____ times; but God suffered him not to hurt me. ⁸If he said thus, The speckled shall be thy wages; then all the cattle bare speckled: and if he said thus, The ringstraked shall be thy hire; then bare all the cattle ringstraked. ⁹Thus God hath taken away the cattle of your father, and given *them* to me. ¹⁰And it came to pass at the time that the cattle conceived, that I lifted up mine eyes, and saw in a dream, and, behold, the rams which leaped upon the cattle *were* ringstraked, speckled, and grisled. ¹¹And the angel of God spake unto me in a dream, *saying,* Jacob: And I said, Here *am* I. ¹²And he said, Lift up now thine eyes, and see, all the rams which leap upon the cattle *are* ringstraked, speckled, and grisled: for I have seen all that Laban doeth unto thee. ¹³I *am* the God of _____, where thou anointedst the pillar, *and* where thou vowedst a vow unto me: now arise, get thee out from this land, and return unto the land of thy kindred. ¹⁴And Rachel and Leah answered and said unto him, *Is there* yet any portion or inheritance for us in our father's house? ¹⁵Are we not counted of him strangers? for he hath sold us, and hath quite devoured also our money. ¹⁶For all the riches which God hath taken from our father, that *is* ours, and our children's: now then, whatsoever God hath said unto thee, do.

¹⁷Then Jacob rose up, and set his sons and his wives upon camels; ¹⁸And he carried away all his cattle, and all his goods which he had gotten, the cattle of his getting, which he had gotten in Padan-aram, for to go to Isaac his father in the land of Canaan. ¹⁹And Laban went to shear his sheep: and Rachel had _____ the _____ that *were* her father's. ²⁰And Jacob stole away unawares to Laban the Syrian, in that he told him not that he fled. ²¹So he fled with all that he had; and he rose up, and passed over the river, and set his face *toward* the mount Gilead. ²²And it was told Laban on the third day that Jacob was fled. ²³And he took his brethren with him, and pursued after him seven days' journey; and they overtook him in the mount Gilead. ²⁴And God came to Laban the

GENESIS

Syrian in a dream by night, and said unto him, Take heed that thou speak not to Jacob either good or bad.

²⁵Then Laban overtook Jacob. Now Jacob had pitched his tent in the mount: and Laban with his brethren pitched in the mount of Gilead. ²⁶And Laban said to Jacob, What hast thou done, that thou hast stolen away unawares to me, and carried away my daughters, as captives *taken* with the sword? ²⁷Wherefore didst thou flee away secretly, and steal away from me; and didst not tell me, that I might have sent thee away with mirth, and with songs, with tabret, and with harp? ²⁸And hast not suffered me to kiss my sons and my daughters? thou hast now done foolishly in so doing. ²⁹It is in the power of my hand to do you hurt: but the God of your father spake unto me yesternight, saying, Take thou heed that thou speak not to Jacob either good or bad. ³⁰And now, *though* thou wouldest needs be gone, because thou sore longedst after thy father's house, *yet* wherefore hast thou stolen my gods? ³¹And Jacob answered and said to Laban, Because I was afraid: for I said, Peradventure thou wouldest take by force thy daughters from me. ³²With whomsoever thou findest thy gods, let him not live: before our brethren discern thou what *is* thine with me, and take *it* to thee. For Jacob knew not that Rachel had stolen them. ³³And Laban went into Jacob's tent, and into Leah's tent, and into the two maidservants' tents; but he found *them* not. Then went he out of Leah's tent, and entered into Rachel's tent. ³⁴Now Rachel had taken the images, and put them in the camel's furniture, and sat upon them. And Laban searched all the tent, but found *them* not. ³⁵And she said to her father, Let it not displease my lord that I cannot rise up before thee; for the custom of women is upon me. And he searched, but found not the images.

³⁶And Jacob was wroth, and chode with Laban: and Jacob answered and said to Laban, What *is* my trespass? what *is* my sin, that thou hast so hotly pursued after me? ³⁷Whereas thou hast searched all my stuff, what hast thou found of all thy household stuff? set *it* here before my brethren and thy brethren, that they may judge betwixt us both. ³⁸This twenty years *have* I *been* with thee; thy ewes and thy she goats have not cast their young, and the rams of thy flock have I not eaten. ³⁹That which was torn *of beasts* I brought not unto thee; I bare the loss of it; of my hand didst thou require it, *whether* stolen by day, or stolen by night. ⁴⁰*Thus* I was; in the day the drought consumed me, and the frost by night; and my sleep departed from mine eyes. ⁴¹Thus have I been twenty years in thy house; I served thee fourteen years for thy two daughters, and six years for thy cattle: and thou hast changed my wages _____ times. ⁴²Except the God of my father, the God of Abraham, and the fear of Isaac, had been with me, surely thou hadst sent me away now empty. God hath seen mine affliction and the labour of my hands, and rebuked *thee* yesternight.

⁴³And Laban answered and said unto Jacob, *These* daughters *are* my daughters, and *these* children *are* my children, and *these* cattle *are* my cattle, and all that thou seest *is* mine: and what can I do this day unto these my daughters, or unto their children which they have born? ⁴⁴Now therefore come thou, let us make a covenant, I and thou; and let it be for a witness between me and thee. ⁴⁵And Jacob took a stone, and set it up *for* a pillar. ⁴⁶And Jacob said unto his brethren, Gather stones; and they took stones, and made an heap: and they did eat there upon the heap. ⁴⁷And Laban called it Jegar-sahadutha: but Jacob called it Galeed. ⁴⁸And Laban said, This heap *is* a witness between me and thee this day. Therefore was the name of it called Galeed; ⁴⁹And Mizpah; for he said, The LORD _____ between me and thee, when we are _____ one from another. ⁵⁰If thou shalt

GENESIS

afflict my daughters, or if thou shalt take *other* wives beside my daughters, no man *is* with us; see, God *is* witness betwixt me and thee. ⁵¹And Laban said to Jacob, Behold this heap, and behold *this* pillar, which I have cast betwixt me and thee; ⁵²This heap *be* witness, and *this* pillar *be* witness, that I will not pass over this heap to thee, and that thou shalt not pass over this heap and this pillar unto me, for harm. ⁵³The God of Abraham, and the God of Nahor, the God of their father, judge betwixt us. And Jacob sware by the _____ of his _____ Isaac. ⁵⁴Then Jacob offered sacrifice upon the mount, and called his brethren to eat bread: and they did eat bread, and tarried all night in the mount. ⁵⁵And early in the morning Laban rose up, and kissed his sons and his daughters, and blessed them: and Laban departed, and returned unto his place.

³²:¹And Jacob went on his way, and the angels of God met him. ²And when Jacob saw them, he said, This *is* God's host: and he called the name of that place Mahanaim. ³And Jacob sent messengers before him to Esau his brother unto the land of Seir, the country of Edom. ⁴And he commanded them, saying, Thus shall ye speak unto my lord Esau; Thy servant Jacob saith thus, I have sojourned with Laban, and stayed there until now: ⁵And I have oxen, and asses, flocks, and menservants, and womenservants: and I have sent to tell my lord, that I may find grace in thy sight.

⁶And the messengers returned to Jacob, saying, We came to thy brother Esau, and also he cometh to meet thee, and four hundred men with him. ⁷Then Jacob was greatly afraid and distressed: and he divided the people that *was* with him, and the flocks, and herds, and the camels, into two bands; ⁸And said, If Esau come to the one company, and smite it, then the other company which is left shall escape.

⁹And Jacob said, O God of my father Abraham, and God of my father Isaac, the LORD which saidst unto me, Return unto thy country, and to thy kindred, and I will deal well with thee: ¹⁰I am not worthy of the least of all the mercies, and of all the truth, which thou hast shewed unto thy servant; for with my _____ I passed over this Jordan; and now I am become two bands. ¹¹Deliver me, I pray thee, from the hand of my brother, from the hand of Esau: for I fear him, lest he will come and smite me, *and* the mother with the children. ¹²And thou saidst, I will surely do thee good, and make thy seed as the sand of the sea, which cannot be numbered for multitude. ¹³And he lodged there that same night; and took of that which came to his hand a present for Esau his brother; ¹⁴Two hundred she goats, and twenty he goats, two hundred ewes, and twenty rams, ¹⁵Thirty milch camels with their colts, forty kine, and ten bulls, twenty she asses, and ten foals. ¹⁶And he delivered *them* into the hand of his servants, every drove by themselves; and said unto his servants, Pass over before me, and put a space betwixt drove and drove. ¹⁷And he commanded the foremost, saying, When Esau my brother meeteth thee, and asketh thee, saying, Whose *art* thou? and whither goest thou? and whose *are* these before thee? ¹⁸Then thou shalt say, *They be* thy servant Jacob's; it *is* a present sent unto my lord Esau: and, behold, also he *is* behind us. ¹⁹And so commanded he the second, and the third, and all that followed the droves, saying, On this manner shall ye speak unto Esau, when ye find him. ²⁰And say ye moreover, Behold, thy servant Jacob *is* behind us. For he said, I will _____ him with the _____ that goeth before me, and afterward I will see his face; peradventure he will accept of me. ²¹So went the present over before him: and himself lodged that night in the company. ²²And he rose up that night, and took his two wives, and his two womenservants, and his eleven sons, and passed over the ford Jabbok. ²³And he took them, and sent them over the brook, and sent over that he had.

²⁴And Jacob was left alone; and there wrestled a man with him until the breaking of the day. ²⁵And when he saw that he prevailed not against him, he touched the _____ of his _____; and the hollow of Jacob's thigh was out of _____, as he wrestled with him. ²⁶And he said, Let me go, for the day breaketh. And he said, I will not let thee go, except thou _____ me. ²⁷And he said unto him, What *is* thy _____? And he said, _____. ²⁸And he said, Thy name shall be called no more Jacob, but _____: for as a _____ hast thou power with God and with men, and hast _____. ²⁹And Jacob asked *him,* and said, Tell *me,* I pray thee, thy name. And he said, Wherefore *is it that* thou dost ask after my name? And he blessed him there. ³⁰And Jacob called the name of the place _____: for I have seen God face to face, and my life is preserved. ³¹And as he passed over Penuel the sun rose upon him, and he halted upon his thigh. ³²Therefore the children of Israel eat not *of* the sinew which shrank, which *is* upon the hollow of the thigh, unto this day: because he touched the hollow of Jacob's thigh in the sinew that shrank.

^{33:1}And Jacob lifted up his eyes, and looked, and, behold, Esau came, and with him four hundred men. And he divided the children unto Leah, and unto Rachel, and unto the two handmaids. ²And he put the handmaids and their children foremost, and Leah and her children after, and Rachel and Joseph hindermost. ³And he passed over _____ them, and bowed himself to the ground seven times, until he came near to his brother. ⁴And Esau ran to meet him, and embraced him, and fell on his neck, and kissed him: and they wept. ⁵And he lifted up his eyes, and saw the women and the children; and said, Who *are* those with thee? And he said, The children which God hath graciously given thy servant. ⁶Then the handmaidens came near, they and their children, and they bowed themselves. ⁷And Leah also with her children came near, and bowed themselves: and after came Joseph near and Rachel, and they bowed themselves. ⁸And he said, What *meanest* thou by all this drove which I met? And he said, *These are* to find grace in the sight of my lord. ⁹And Esau said, I have enough, my brother; keep that thou hast unto thyself. ¹⁰And Jacob said, Nay, I pray thee, if now I have found grace in thy sight, then receive my present at my hand: for therefore I have seen thy face, as though I had seen the face of God, and thou wast pleased with me. ¹¹_____, I pray thee, _____ _____ that is brought to thee; because God hath dealt graciously with me, and because I have _____. And he urged him, and he took *it.* ¹²And he said, Let us take our journey, and let us go, and I will go before thee. ¹³And he said unto him, My lord knoweth that the children *are* tender, and the flocks and herds with young *are* with me: and if men should overdrive them one day, all the flock will die. ¹⁴Let my lord, I pray thee, pass over before his servant: and I will lead on softly, according as the cattle that goeth before me and the children be able to endure, until I come unto my lord unto Seir. ¹⁵And Esau said, Let me now leave with thee *some* of the folk that *are* with me. And he said, What needeth it? let me find grace in the sight of my lord.

¹⁶So Esau returned that day on his way unto Seir. ¹⁷And Jacob journeyed to Succoth, and built him an house, and made booths for his cattle: therefore the name of the place is called Succoth.

¹⁸And Jacob came to Shalem, a city of Shechem, which *is* in the land of Canaan, when he came from Padan-aram; and pitched his tent before the city. ¹⁹And he bought a parcel of a field, where he had spread his tent, at the hand of the children of Hamor, Shechem's

father, for an hundred pieces of money. ²⁰And he erected there an altar, and called it
_____-_____-_____.

   ³⁴:¹And Dinah the daughter of Leah, which she bare unto Jacob, went _____to
_____the daughters of the land. ²And when _____the son of Hamor the Hivite,
prince of the country, _____her, he _____her, and lay with her, and _____her.
³And his soul clave unto Dinah the daughter of Jacob, and he loved the damsel, and spake
kindly unto the damsel. ⁴And Shechem spake unto his father Hamor, saying, Get me this
damsel to wife. ⁵And Jacob heard that he had _____Dinah his daughter: now his sons
were with his cattle in the field: and Jacob held his peace until they were come.

   ⁶And Hamor the father of Shechem went out unto Jacob to commune with him. ⁷And
the sons of Jacob came out of the field when they heard *it:* and the men were _____,
and they were very _____, because he had wrought _____in Israel in lying with
Jacob's daughter; which thing ought _____to be done. ⁸And Hamor communed with
them, saying, The soul of my son Shechem longeth for your daughter: I pray you give her
him to wife. ⁹And make ye marriages with us, *and* give your daughters unto us, and take
our daughters unto you. ¹⁰And ye shall dwell with us: and the land shall be before you;
dwell and trade ye therein, and get you possessions therein. ¹¹And Shechem said unto her
father and unto her brethren, Let me find grace in your eyes, and what ye shall say unto
me I will give. ¹²Ask me never so much dowry and gift, and I will give according as ye
shall say unto me: but give me the damsel to wife. ¹³And the sons of Jacob answered
Shechem and Hamor his father _____, and said, because he had _____Dinah their
sister: ¹⁴And they said unto them, We cannot do this thing, to give our sister to one that is
uncircumcised; for that *were* a reproach unto us: ¹⁵But in this will we consent unto you: If
ye will be as we *be,* that every male of you be circumcised; ¹⁶Then will we give our
daughters unto you, and we will take your daughters to us, and we will dwell with you,
and we will become one people. ¹⁷But if ye will not hearken unto us, to be circumcised;
then will we take our daughter, and we will be gone. ¹⁸And their words pleased Hamor,
and Shechem Hamor's son. ¹⁹And the young man deferred not to do the thing, because he
had delight in Jacob's daughter: and he *was* more _____than all the house of his
father.

   ²⁰And Hamor and Shechem his son came unto the gate of their city, and communed
with the men of their city, saying, ²¹These men *are* peaceable with us; therefore let them
dwell in the land, and trade therein; for the land, behold, *it is* large enough for them; let
us _____their daughters to us for wives, and let us give them our daughters. ²²Only
herein will the men consent unto us for to dwell with us, to be one people, if every male
among us be circumcised, as they *are* circumcised. ²³*Shall* not their _____and their
_____and every _____of theirs *be* _____? only let us consent unto them, and
they will dwell with us. ²⁴And unto Hamor and unto Shechem his son hearkened all that
went out of the gate of his city; and every male was circumcised, all that went out of the
gate of his city.

   ²⁵And it came to pass on the third day, when they were sore, that two of the sons of
Jacob, Simeon and Levi, Dinah's brethren, took each man his sword, and came upon the
city boldly, and slew all the males. ²⁶And they slew Hamor and Shechem his son with the
edge of the sword, and took Dinah out of Shechem's house, and went out. ²⁷The sons of
Jacob came upon the slain, and spoiled the city, because they had _____their sister.
²⁸They took their sheep, and their oxen, and their asses, and that which *was* in the city,

GENESIS

and that which *was* in the field, ²⁹And all their wealth, and all their little ones, and their wives took they captive, and spoiled even all that *was* in the house. ³⁰And Jacob said to Simeon and Levi, Ye have troubled me to make me to stink among the inhabitants of the land, among the Canaanites and the Perizzites: and I *being* few in number, they shall gather themselves together against me, and slay me; and I shall be destroyed, I and my house. ³¹And they said, _____ he _____ with our _____ as with an _____?

³⁵:¹And God said unto Jacob, Arise, _____ up to _____, and _____ there: and make there an altar unto God, that appeared unto thee when thou fleddest from the face of Esau thy brother. ²Then Jacob said unto his household, and to all that *were* with him, Put away the strange gods that *are* among you, and be _____, and change your _____: ³And let us arise, and go up to Bethel; and I will make there an altar unto God, who answered me in the day of my _____, and was _____ me in the _____ which I went. ⁴And they gave unto Jacob all the strange gods which *were* in their hand, and *all their* earrings which *were* in their ears; and Jacob hid them under the oak which *was* by Shechem. ⁵And they journeyed: and the terror of God was upon the cities that *were* round about them, and they did not pursue after the sons of Jacob.

⁶So Jacob came to Luz, which *is* in the land of Canaan, that *is,* Bethel, he and all the people that *were* with him. ⁷And he built there an altar, and called the place El-beth-el: because there God appeared unto him, when he fled from the face of his brother. ⁸But Deborah Rebekah's nurse died, and she was buried beneath Bethel under an oak: and the name of it was called Allon-bachuth.

⁹And God appeared unto Jacob again, when he came out of Padan-aram, and blessed him. ¹⁰And God said unto him, Thy name *is* Jacob: thy name shall not be called any more Jacob, but _____ shall be thy name: and he called his name _____. ¹¹And God said unto him, I *am* God Almighty: be fruitful and multiply; a nation and a company of nations shall be of thee, and kings shall come out of thy loins; ¹²And the land which I gave Abraham and Isaac, to thee I will give it, and to thy seed after thee will I give the land. ¹³And God went up from him in the place where he talked with him. ¹⁴And Jacob set up a pillar in the place where he talked with him, *even* a pillar of stone: and he poured a drink offering thereon, and he poured oil thereon. ¹⁵And Jacob called the name of the place where God spake with him, Bethel.

¹⁶And they journeyed from Bethel; and there was but a little way to come to Ephrath: and Rachel travailed, and she had hard labour. ¹⁷And it came to pass, when she was in hard labour, that the midwife said unto her, Fear not; thou shalt have this son also. ¹⁸And it came to pass, as her soul was in departing, (for she _____) that she called his name _____-_____: but his father called him _____. ¹⁹And Rachel died, and was buried in the way to Ephrath, which *is* Bethlehem. ²⁰And Jacob set a pillar upon her grave: that *is* the pillar of Rachel's grave unto this day.

²¹And Israel journeyed, and spread his tent beyond the tower of Edar. ²²And it came to pass, when Israel dwelt in that land, that Reuben went and lay with Bilhah his father's concubine: and Israel heard *it.* Now the sons of Jacob were twelve: ²³The sons of Leah; _____, Jacob's firstborn, and _____, and _____, and _____, and _____, and _____: ²⁴The sons of _____; _____, and _____: ²⁵And the sons of _____, Rachel's _____; _____, and _____: ²⁶And the sons of _____, Leah's _____; _____, and _____: these *are* the sons of Jacob, which were born to him in Padan-aram.

By Faith Publications

37

^{27}And Jacob came unto Isaac his father unto Mamre, unto the city of Arbah, which *is* Hebron, where Abraham and Isaac sojourned. ^{28}And the days of Isaac were an hundred and fourscore years. ^{29}And Isaac gave up the ghost, and died, and was gathered unto his people, *being* old and full of days: and his sons Esau and Jacob buried him.

$^{36:1}$Now these *are* the generations of Esau, who *is* _____. ^{2}Esau took his wives of the daughters of Canaan; Adah the daughter of Elon the Hittite, and Aholibamah the daughter of Anah the daughter of Zibeon the Hivite; ^{3}And Bashemath Ishmael's daughter, sister of Nebajoth. ^{4}And Adah bare to Esau Eliphaz; and Bashemath bare Reuel; ^{5}And Aholibamah bare Jeush, and Jaalam, and Korah: these *are* the sons of Esau, which were born unto him in the land of Canaan. ^{6}And Esau took his wives, and his sons, and his daughters, and all the persons of his house, and his cattle, and all his beasts, and all his substance, which he had got in the land of Canaan; and went into the country from the face of his brother Jacob. ^{7}For their riches were more than that they might dwell together; and the land wherein they were strangers could not bear them because of their cattle. ^{8}Thus dwelt Esau in mount Seir: Esau *is* Edom.

^{9}And these *are* the generations of Esau the father of the Edomites in mount Seir: ^{10}These *are* the names of Esau's sons; Eliphaz the son of Adah the wife of Esau, Reuel the son of Bashemath the wife of Esau. ^{11}And the sons of Eliphaz were Teman, Omar, Zepho, and Gatam, and Kenaz. ^{12}And Timna was concubine to Eliphaz Esau's son; and she bare to Eliphaz Amalek: these *were* the sons of Adah Esau's wife. ^{13}And these *are* the sons of Reuel; Nahath, and Zerah, Shammah, and Mizzah: these were the sons of Bashemath Esau's wife.

^{14}And these were the sons of Aholibamah, the daughter of Anah the daughter of Zibeon, Esau's wife: and she bare to Esau Jeush, and Jaalam, and Korah.

^{15}These *were* dukes of the sons of Esau: the sons of Eliphaz the firstborn *son* of Esau; duke Teman, duke Omar, duke Zepho, duke Kenaz, ^{16}Duke Korah, duke Gatam, *and* duke Amalek: these *are* the dukes *that came* of Eliphaz in the land of Edom; these *were* the sons of Adah.

^{17}And these *are* the sons of Reuel Esau's son; duke Nahath, duke Zerah, duke Shammah, duke Mizzah: these *are* the dukes *that came* of Reuel in the land of Edom; these *are* the sons of Bashemath Esau's wife.

^{18}And these *are* the sons of Aholibamah Esau's wife; duke Jeush, duke Jaalam, duke Korah: these *were* the dukes *that came* of Aholibamah the daughter of Anah, Esau's wife. ^{19}These *are* the sons of Esau, who *is* Edom, and these *are* their dukes.

^{20}These *are* the sons of Seir the Horite, who inhabited the land; Lotan, and Shobal, and Zibeon, and Anah, ^{21}And Dishon, and Ezer, and Dishan: these *are* the dukes of the Horites, the children of Seir in the land of Edom. ^{22}And the children of Lotan were Hori and Hemam; and Lotan's sister *was* Timna. ^{23}And the children of Shobal *were* these; Alvan, and Manahath, and Ebal, Shepho, and Onam. ^{24}And these *are* the children of Zibeon; both Ajah, and Anah: this *was that* Anah that _____ the _____ in the _____, as he fed the _____ of Zibeon his father. ^{25}And the children of Anah *were* these; Dishon, and Aholibamah the daughter of Anah. ^{26}And these *are* the children of Dishon; Hemdan, and Eshban, and Ithran, and Cheran. ^{27}The children of Ezer *are* these; Bilhan, and Zaavan, and Akan. ^{28}The children of Dishan *are* these: Uz, and Aran. ^{29}These *are* the dukes *that came* of the Horites; duke Lotan, duke Shobal, duke Zibeon, duke

Anah, ³⁰Duke Dishon, duke Ezer, duke Dishan: these *are* the dukes *that came* of Hori, among their dukes in the land of Seir.

³¹And these *are* the kings that reigned in the land of Edom, before there reigned any king over the children of Israel. ³²And Bela the son of Beor reigned in Edom: and the name of his city *was* Dinhabah. ³³And Bela died, and Jobab the son of Zerah of Bozrah reigned in his stead. ³⁴And Jobab died, and Husham of the land of Temani reigned in his stead. ³⁵And Husham died, and Hadad the son of Bedad, who smote Midian in the field of Moab, reigned in his stead: and the name of his city *was* Avith. ³⁶And Hadad died, and Samlah of Masrekah reigned in his stead. ³⁷And Samlah died, and Saul of Rehoboth *by* the river reigned in his stead. ³⁸And Saul died, and Baal-hanan the son of Achbor reigned in his stead. ³⁹And Baal-hanan the son of Achbor died, and Hadar reigned in his stead: and the name of his city *was* Pau; and his wife's name *was* Mehetabel, the daughter of Matred, the daughter of Mezahab. ⁴⁰And these *are* the names of the dukes *that came* of Esau, according to their families, after their places, by their names; duke Timnah, duke Alvah, duke Jetheth, ⁴¹Duke Aholibamah, duke Elah, duke Pinon, ⁴²Duke Kenaz, duke Teman, duke Mibzar, ⁴³Duke Magdiel, duke Iram: these *be* the dukes of Edom, according to their habitations in the land of their possession: he *is* Esau the father of the Edomites.

³⁷:¹And Jacob dwelt in the land wherein his father was a _____, in the land of Canaan. ²These *are* the generations of Jacob. Joseph, *being* _____years old, was feeding the flock with his brethren; and the lad *was* with the sons of Bilhah, and with the sons of Zilpah, his father's wives: and Joseph brought unto his father their _____report. ³Now Israel _____Joseph _____than all his children, because he *was* the son of his old age: and he made him a _____of *many* _____. ⁴And when his brethren saw that their father loved him more than all his brethren, they _____him, and could not speak _____unto him.

⁵And Joseph _____a dream, and he told *it* his brethren: and they hated him yet the more. ⁶And he said unto them, Hear, I pray you, this dream which I have dreamed: ⁷For, behold, we *were* binding _____in the field, and, lo, my sheaf arose, and also stood upright; and, behold, your sheaves stood round about, and made _____to my sheaf. ⁸And his brethren said to him, Shalt thou indeed _____over us? or shalt thou indeed have dominion over us? And they hated him yet the more for his dreams, and for his words.

⁹And he dreamed yet another dream, and told it his brethren, and said, Behold, I have dreamed a dream more; and, behold, the _____and the _____and the _____made _____to me. ¹⁰And he told *it* to his father, and to his brethren: and his father rebuked him, and said unto him, What *is* this dream that thou hast dreamed? Shall I and thy mother and thy brethren indeed come to bow down ourselves to thee to the earth? ¹¹And his brethren _____him; but his father observed the saying.

¹²And his brethren went to feed their father's flock in Shechem. ¹³And Israel said unto Joseph, Do not thy brethren feed *the flock* in Shechem? come, and I will send thee unto them. And he said to him, Here *am* I. ¹⁴And he said to him, Go, I pray thee, see whether it be well with thy brethren, and well with the flocks; and bring me word again. So he sent him out of the vale of Hebron, and he came to Shechem.

¹⁵And a certain man found him, and, behold, *he was* wandering in the field: and the man asked him, saying, What seekest thou? ¹⁶And he said, I seek my brethren: tell me, I pray thee, where they feed *their flocks*. ¹⁷And the man said, They are departed hence; for

I heard them say, Let us go to Dothan. And Joseph went after his brethren, and found them in Dothan. ¹⁸And when they saw him afar off, even before he came near unto them, they _____against him to _____him. ¹⁹And they said one to another, Behold, this _____cometh. ²⁰Come now therefore, and let us _____him, and cast him into some _____, and we will say, Some evil beast hath devoured him: and we shall see what will become of his dreams. ²¹And _____heard *it,* and he _____him out of their hands; and said, Let us not kill him. ²²And Reuben said unto them, Shed no blood, *but* cast him into this pit that is in the wilderness, and lay no hand upon him; that he might rid him out of their hands, to deliver him to his father again.

²³And it came to pass, when Joseph was come unto his brethren, that they stript Joseph out of his _____, *his* coat of *many* colours that *was* on him; ²⁴And they took him, and _____him into a _____: and the pit *was* _____, *there was* no _____in it. ²⁵And they sat down to eat bread: and they lifted up their eyes and looked, and, behold, a company of Ishmeelites came from Gilead with their camels bearing spicery and balm and myrrh, going to carry *it* down to Egypt. ²⁶And Judah said unto his brethren, What _____*is it* if we slay our brother, and conceal his blood? ²⁷Come, and let us _____him to the _____, and let not our hand be upon him; for he *is* our brother *and* our flesh. And his brethren were content. ²⁸Then there passed by Midianites merchantmen; and they drew and lifted up Joseph out of the pit, and _____Joseph to the Ishmeelites for _____*pieces* of _____: and they brought Joseph into _____.

²⁹And Reuben returned unto the pit; and, behold, Joseph *was* not in the pit; and he rent his clothes. ³⁰And he returned unto his brethren, and said, The child *is* not; and I, whither shall I go? ³¹And they took Joseph's coat, and killed a kid of the goats, and dipped the coat in the blood; ³²And they sent the coat of *many* colours, and they brought *it* to their father; and said, This have we found: know now whether it *be* thy son's coat or no. ³³And he knew it, and said, *It is* my son's coat; an evil beast hath devoured him; Joseph is without doubt rent in pieces. ³⁴And Jacob rent his clothes, and put sackcloth upon his loins, and mourned for his son many days. ³⁵And all his sons and all his daughters rose up to comfort him; but he refused to be comforted; and he said, For I will go down into the grave unto my son mourning. Thus his father wept for him. ³⁶And the _____sold him into Egypt unto _____, an officer of _____, *and* _____of the _____.

³⁸:¹And it came to pass at that time, that Judah went down from his brethren, and turned in to a certain Adullamite, whose name *was* Hirah. ²And Judah saw there a daughter of a certain Canaanite, whose name *was* Shuah; and he took her, and went in unto her. ³And she conceived, and bare a son; and he called his name Er. ⁴And she conceived again, and bare a son; and she called his name _____. ⁵And she yet again conceived, and bare a son; and called his name Shelah: and he was at Chezib, when she bare him. ⁶And Judah took a wife for Er his firstborn, whose name *was* _____. ⁷And Er, Judah's firstborn, was wicked in the sight of the LORD; and the LORD _____him. ⁸And Judah said unto Onan, Go in unto thy brother's wife, and marry her, and raise up seed to thy brother. ⁹And Onan _____that the _____should not be his; and it came to pass, when he went in unto his brother's wife, that he _____*it* on the ground, lest that he should give seed to his _____. ¹⁰And the thing which he did _____the LORD: wherefore he _____him also. ¹¹Then said Judah to Tamar his daughter in law, Remain a widow at

thy father's house, till Shelah my son be grown: for he said, Lest peradventure he die also, as his brethren *did.* And Tamar went and dwelt in her father's house.

¹²And in process of time the daughter of Shuah Judah's wife died; and Judah was comforted, and went up unto his sheepshearers to Timnath, he and his friend Hirah the Adullamite. ¹³And it was told Tamar, saying, Behold thy father in law goeth up to Timnath to shear his sheep. ¹⁴And she put her widow's garments off from her, and covered her with a vail, and wrapped herself, and sat in an open place, which *is* by the way to Timnath; for she saw that Shelah was grown, and she was not given unto him to wife. ¹⁵When Judah _____ her, he _____ her *to be* an _____; _____ she had _____ her _____. ¹⁶And he turned unto her by the way, and said, Go to, I pray thee, let me come in unto thee; (for he knew not that she *was* his daughter in law.) And she said, What wilt thou give me, that thou mayest come in unto me? ¹⁷And he said, I will send *thee* a kid from the flock. And she said, Wilt thou give *me* a pledge, till thou send *it?* ¹⁸And he said, What pledge shall I give thee? And she said, Thy signet, and thy bracelets, and thy staff that *is* in thine hand. And he gave *it* her, and came in unto her, and she conceived by him. ¹⁹And she arose, and went away, and laid by her vail from her, and put on the garments of her widowhood. ²⁰And Judah sent the kid by the hand of his friend the Adullamite, to receive *his* pledge from the woman's hand: but he found her not. ²¹Then he asked the men of that place, saying, Where *is* the harlot, that *was* openly by the way side? And they said, There was no harlot in this *place.* ²²And he returned to Judah, and said, I cannot find her; and also the men of the place said, *that* there was no harlot in this *place.* ²³And Judah said, Let her take *it* to her, lest we be shamed: behold, I sent this kid, and thou hast not found her.

²⁴And it came to pass about three months after, that it was told Judah, saying, Tamar thy daughter in law hath played the harlot; and also, behold, she *is* with child by whoredom. And Judah said, Bring her forth, and let her be burnt. ²⁵When she *was* brought forth, she sent to her father in law, saying, By the man, whose these *are, am* I with child: and she said, Discern, I pray thee, whose *are* these, the signet, and bracelets, and staff. ²⁶And Judah acknowledged *them,* and said, She hath been more righteous than I; because that I gave her not to Shelah my son. And he knew her again _____ more.

²⁷And it came to pass in the time of her travail, that, behold, _____ *were* in her womb. ²⁸And it came to pass, when she travailed, that *the one* put out *his* hand: and the midwife took and bound upon his hand a _____ _____, saying, This came out _____, ²⁹And it came to pass, as he drew back his hand, that, behold, his brother came out: and she said, How hast thou broken forth? *this* breach *be* upon thee: therefore his name was called Pharez. ³⁰And afterward came out his brother, that had the scarlet thread upon his hand: and his name was called Zarah.

³⁹:¹And _____ was brought _____ to _____; and Potiphar, an officer of Pharaoh, captain of the guard, an Egyptian, bought him of the hands of the Ishmeelites, which had brought him down thither. ²And the LORD was _____ Joseph, and he was a _____ man; and he was in the house of his master the Egyptian. ³And his master _____ that the LORD *was* with him, and that the LORD _____ all *that* he did to _____ in his hand. ⁴And Joseph found _____ in his sight, and he _____ him: and he made him _____ over his house, and all that he had he put into his hand. ⁵And it came to pass from the time *that* he had made him overseer in his house, and over all that he had, that the LORD _____ the Egyptian's house for _____ sake; and the

blessing of the LORD was upon all that he had in the house, and in the field. ⁶And he left all that he had in Joseph's hand; and he knew not ought he had, save the bread which he did eat. And Joseph was a _____ *person,* and well favoured.

⁷And it came to pass after these things, that his master's wife cast her eyes upon Joseph; and she said, Lie with me. ⁸But he _____, and said unto his master's wife, Behold, my master wotteth not what *is* with me in the house, and he hath committed all that he hath to my hand; ⁹*There is* none greater in this house than I; neither hath he kept back any thing from me but thee, because thou *art* his _____: how then can I do this _____ _____, and _____ against _____? ¹⁰And it came to pass, as she spake to Joseph day by day, that he hearkened _____ unto her, to lie by her, *or* to _____ with her. ¹¹And it came to pass about this time, that *Joseph* went into the house to do his business; and *there was* none of the men of the house there within. ¹²And she caught him by his garment, saying, Lie with me: and he _____ his _____ in her hand, and fled, and got him _____. ¹³And it came to pass, when she saw that he had left his garment in her hand, and was fled forth, ¹⁴That she called unto the men of her house, and spake unto them, saying, See, he hath brought in an Hebrew unto us to mock us; he came in unto me to lie with me, and I cried with a loud voice: ¹⁵And it came to pass, when he heard that I lifted up my voice and cried, that he left his garment with me, and fled, and got him out. ¹⁶And she laid up his garment by her, until his lord came home. ¹⁷And she spake unto him according to these words, saying, The Hebrew servant, which thou hast brought unto us, came in unto me to mock me: ¹⁸And it came to pass, as I lifted up my voice and cried, that he left his garment with me, and fled out. ¹⁹And it came to pass, when his master heard the words of his wife, which she spake unto him, saying, After this manner did thy servant to me; that his wrath was kindled. ²⁰And Joseph's master took him, and put him into the _____, a place where the king's prisoners *were* bound: and he was there in the prison.

²¹But the _____ was _____ Joseph, and shewed him _____, and gave him _____ in the sight of the _____ of the prison. ²²And the keeper of the prison _____ to Joseph's hand all the _____ that *were* in the prison; and whatsoever they _____ there, he was the _____ *of it.* ²³The keeper of the prison looked not to any thing *that was* under his hand; because the LORD was _____ him, and *that* which he did, the LORD made *it* to _____.

⁴⁰:¹And it came to pass after these things, *that* the _____ of the king of Egypt and *his* _____ had _____ their lord the king of Egypt. ²And Pharaoh was wroth against two *of* his officers, against the chief of the butlers, and against the chief of the bakers. ³And he put them in ward in the house of the _____ of the _____, into the prison, the place where Joseph *was* bound. ⁴And the _____ of the _____ charged Joseph with them, and he _____ them: and they continued a season in ward.

⁵And they _____ a dream both of them, each man his dream in one night, each man according to the interpretation of his dream, the butler and the baker of the king of Egypt, which *were* bound in the prison. ⁶And Joseph came in unto them in the morning, and looked upon them, and, behold, they *were* sad. ⁷And he asked Pharaoh's officers that *were* with him in the ward of his lord's house, saying, Wherefore look ye *so* sadly to day? ⁸And they said unto him, We have dreamed a dream, and *there is* no interpreter of it. And Joseph said unto them, *Do* not _____ *belong* to _____? tell me *them,* I pray you. ⁹And the chief butler told his dream to Joseph, and said to him, In my dream, behold, a

vine *was* before me; ¹⁰And in the vine *were* three branches: and it *was* as though it budded, *and* her blossoms shot forth; and the clusters thereof brought forth ripe grapes: ¹¹And Pharaoh's cup *was* in my hand: and I took the grapes, and pressed them into Pharaoh's cup, and I gave the cup into Pharaoh's hand. ¹²And Joseph said unto him, This *is* the interpretation of it: The three branches *are* three days: ¹³Yet within three days shall Pharaoh lift up thine head, and restore thee unto thy place: and thou shalt deliver Pharaoh's cup into his hand, after the former manner when thou wast his butler. ¹⁴But _____ on _____ when it shall be _____ with _____, and shew _____, I pray thee, unto me, and make _____ of me unto Pharaoh, and bring me _____ of this house: ¹⁵For indeed I was stolen away out of the land of the Hebrews: and here also have I done nothing that they should put me into the dungeon. ¹⁶When the chief baker saw that the interpretation was good, he said unto Joseph, I also *was* in my dream, and, behold, *I had* three white baskets on my head: ¹⁷And in the uppermost basket *there was* of all manner of bakemeats for Pharaoh; and the birds did eat them out of the basket upon my head. ¹⁸And Joseph answered and said, This *is* the interpretation thereof: The three baskets *are* three days: ¹⁹Yet within three days shall Pharaoh lift up thy head from off thee, and shall hang thee on a tree; and the birds shall eat thy flesh from off thee.

²⁰And it came to pass the third day, *which was* Pharaoh's _____, that he made a feast unto all his servants: and he lifted up the head of the chief butler and of the chief baker among his servants. ²¹And he restored the chief butler unto his butlership again; and he gave the cup into Pharaoh's hand: ²²But he hanged the chief baker: as Joseph had interpreted to them. ²³Yet did _____ the chief butler remember Joseph, but _____ him.

⁴¹:¹And it came to pass at the end of _____ full _____, that Pharaoh _____: and, behold, he stood by the river. ²And, behold, there came up out of the river seven well favoured kine and fatfleshed; and they fed in a meadow. ³And, behold, seven other kine came up after them out of the river, ill favoured and leanfleshed; and stood by the *other* kine upon the brink of the river. ⁴And the ill favoured and leanfleshed kine did eat up the seven well favoured and fat kine. So Pharaoh awoke. ⁵And he slept and dreamed the second time: and, behold, seven ears of corn came up upon one stalk, rank and good. ⁶And, behold, seven thin ears and blasted with the east wind sprung up after them. ⁷And the seven thin ears devoured the seven rank and full ears. And Pharaoh awoke, and, behold, *it was* a dream. ⁸And it came to pass in the morning that his spirit was troubled; and he sent and called for all the magicians of Egypt, and all the wise men thereof: and Pharaoh told them his dream; but *there was* none that could interpret them unto Pharaoh.

⁹Then spake the chief butler unto Pharaoh, saying, I do remember my faults this day: ¹⁰Pharaoh was wroth with his servants, and put me in ward in the captain of the guard's house, both *me* and the chief baker: ¹¹And we dreamed a dream in one night, I and he; we dreamed each man according to the interpretation of his dream. ¹²And *there was* there with us a young man, an Hebrew, servant to the captain of the guard; and we told him, and he interpreted to us our dreams; to each man according to his dream he did interpret. ¹³And it came to pass, as he interpreted to us, so it was; me he restored unto mine office, and him he hanged.

¹⁴Then Pharaoh sent and called Joseph, and they brought him hastily out of the dungeon: and he shaved *himself,* and changed his raiment, and came in unto Pharaoh. ¹⁵And Pharaoh said unto Joseph, I have dreamed a dream, and *there is* none that can

GENESIS

interpret it: and I have heard say of thee, *that* thou canst understand a dream to interpret it. ¹⁶And Joseph answered Pharaoh, saying, *It is* _____ in _____ : _____ shall give Pharaoh an answer of _____ . ¹⁷And Pharaoh said unto Joseph, In my dream, behold, I stood upon the bank of the river: ¹⁸And, behold, there came up out of the river seven kine, fatfleshed and well favoured; and they fed in a meadow: ¹⁹And, behold, seven other kine came up after them, poor and very ill favoured and leanfleshed, such as I never saw in all the land of Egypt for badness: ²⁰And the lean and the ill favoured kine did eat up the first seven fat kine: ²¹And when they had eaten them up, it could not be known that they had eaten them; but they *were* still ill favoured, as at the beginning. So I awoke. ²²And I saw in my dream, and, behold, seven ears came up in one stalk, full and good: ²³And, behold, seven ears, withered, thin, *and* blasted with the _____ wind, sprung up after them: ²⁴And the thin ears devoured the seven good ears: and I told *this* unto the magicians; but *there was* none that could declare *it* to me.

²⁵And Joseph said unto Pharaoh, The dream of Pharaoh *is* one: God hath shewed Pharaoh what he *is* about to _____ . ²⁶The seven good kine *are* seven _____ ; and the seven good ears *are* seven _____ : the dream *is* one. ²⁷And the seven thin and ill favoured kine that came up after them *are* seven _____ ; and the seven empty ears blasted with the east wind shall be seven _____ of _____ . ²⁸This *is* the thing which I have spoken unto Pharaoh: What _____ *is* about to do he sheweth unto Pharaoh. ²⁹Behold, there come seven years of great _____ throughout all the land of Egypt: ³⁰And there shall arise after them seven years of _____ ; and all the plenty shall be forgotten in the land of Egypt; and the famine shall consume the land; ³¹And the plenty shall not be known in the land by reason of that famine following; for it *shall be* very grievous. ³²And for that the dream was _____ unto Pharaoh _____ ; *it is* _____ the thing *is* _____ by God, and God will shortly bring it to pass. ³³Now therefore let Pharaoh look out a man discreet and wise, and set him over the land of Egypt. ³⁴Let Pharaoh do *this,* and let him appoint officers over the land, and take up the _____ part of the land of Egypt in the seven plenteous years. ³⁵And let them gather all the food of those good years that come, and lay up corn under the hand of Pharaoh, and let them keep food in the cities. ³⁶And that food shall be for store to the land against the seven years of famine, which shall be in the land of Egypt; that the land perish not through the famine.

³⁷And the thing was good in the eyes of Pharaoh, and in the eyes of all his servants. ³⁸And Pharaoh said unto his servants, Can we find *such a one* as this *is,* a man in whom the _____ of _____ is? ³⁹And Pharaoh said unto Joseph, Forasmuch as God hath shewed thee all this, *there is* none so discreet and wise as thou *art:* ⁴⁰Thou shalt be over my house, and according unto thy word shall all my people be ruled: only in the throne will I be greater than thou. ⁴¹And Pharaoh said unto Joseph, See, I have set thee over all the land of Egypt. ⁴²And Pharaoh took off his ring from his hand, and put it upon Joseph's hand, and arrayed him in vestures of fine linen, and put a gold chain about his neck; ⁴³And he made him to ride in the second chariot which he had; and they cried before him, Bow the knee: and he made him *ruler* over all the land of Egypt. ⁴⁴And Pharaoh said unto Joseph, I *am* Pharaoh, and without thee shall no man lift up his hand or foot in all the land of Egypt. ⁴⁵And Pharaoh called Joseph's name _____-_____ ; and he gave him to wife _____ the daughter of _____-_____ priest of On. And Joseph went out over *all* the land of Egypt.

GENESIS

⁴⁶And Joseph *was* _____ years old when he stood before Pharaoh king of Egypt. And Joseph went out from the presence of Pharaoh, and went throughout all the land of Egypt. ⁴⁷And in the seven plenteous years the earth brought forth by handfuls. ⁴⁸And he gathered up all the food of the seven years, which were in the land of Egypt, and laid up the food in the cities: the food of the field, which *was* round about every city, laid he up in the same. ⁴⁹And Joseph gathered corn as the sand of the sea, very much, until he left numbering; for *it was* without number. ⁵⁰And unto Joseph were born two sons before the years of famine came, which Asenath the daughter of Poti-pherah priest of On bare unto him. ⁵¹And Joseph called the name of the firstborn _____ : For God, *said he,* hath made me forget all my _____ , and all my father's house. ⁵²And the name of the second called he _____ : For God hath caused me to be _____ in the land of my _____ .

⁵³And the seven years of plenteousness, that was in the land of Egypt, were ended. ⁵⁴And the seven years of dearth began to come, according as Joseph had said: and the dearth was in all lands; but in all the land of Egypt there was bread. ⁵⁵And when all the land of Egypt was famished, the people cried to Pharaoh for bread: and Pharaoh said unto all the Egyptians, Go unto Joseph; what he saith to you, do. ⁵⁶And the famine was over all the face of the earth: and Joseph opened all the storehouses, and sold unto the Egyptians; and the famine waxed sore in the land of Egypt. ⁵⁷And all countries came into Egypt to Joseph for to buy *corn;* because that the famine was so sore in all lands.

⁴²:¹Now when Jacob saw that there was corn in Egypt, Jacob said unto his sons, Why do ye look one upon another? ²And he said, Behold, I have heard that there is corn in Egypt: get you down thither, and buy for us from thence; that we may live, and not die.

³And Joseph's _____ brethren went down to buy corn in Egypt. ⁴But _____ , Joseph's brother, Jacob sent not with his brethren; for he said, Lest peradventure mischief befall him. ⁵And the sons of Israel came to buy *corn* among those that came: for the famine was in the land of Canaan. ⁶And Joseph *was* the _____ over the land, *and* he it *was* that sold to all the people of the land: and Joseph's brethren _____ , and _____ down themselves before him *with* their faces to the earth. ⁷And Joseph saw his brethren, and he knew them, but made himself _____ unto them, and spake _____ unto them; and he said unto them, Whence come ye? And they said, From the land of Canaan to buy food. ⁸And Joseph knew his brethren, but they knew not him. ⁹And Joseph _____ the _____ which he dreamed of them, and said unto them, Ye *are* _____ ; to see the nakedness of the land ye are come. ¹⁰And they said unto him, Nay, my lord, but to buy food are thy servants come. ¹¹We *are* all one man's sons; we *are* true *men,* thy servants are no spies. ¹²And he said unto them, Nay, but to see the nakedness of the land ye are come. ¹³And they said, Thy servants *are* _____ brethren, the sons of one man in the land of Canaan; and, behold, the youngest *is* this day with our father, and one *is* not. ¹⁴And Joseph said unto them, That *is it* that I spake unto you, saying, Ye *are* spies: ¹⁵Hereby ye shall be proved: By the life of Pharaoh ye shall not go forth hence, except your _____ brother come hither. ¹⁶Send one of you, and let him fetch your brother, and ye shall be kept in prison, that your words may be proved, whether *there be any* truth in you: or else by the life of Pharaoh surely ye *are* spies. ¹⁷And he put them all together into ward three days. ¹⁸And Joseph said unto them the third day, This do, and live; *for* I fear _____ : ¹⁹If ye *be* true *men,* let one of your brethren be bound in the house of your prison: go ye, carry corn for the famine of your houses: ²⁰But bring your

youngest brother unto me; so shall your words be verified, and ye shall not die. And they did so.

²¹And they said one to another, We *are* _____ concerning our _____ , in that we saw the _____ of his soul, when he _____ us, and we would _____ hear; therefore is this _____ come upon us. ²²And _____ answered them, saying, Spake I not unto you, saying, Do not _____ against the _____ ; and ye would not hear? therefore, behold, also his blood is required. ²³And they knew not that Joseph understood *them;* for he spake unto them by an interpreter. ²⁴And he turned himself about from them, and _____ ; and returned to them again, and communed with them, and took from them _____ , and bound him before their eyes.

²⁵Then Joseph commanded to fill their sacks with _____ , and to _____ every man's _____ into his sack, and to give them _____ for the way: and thus did he unto them. ²⁶And they laded their asses with the corn, and departed thence. ²⁷And as one of them opened his sack to give his ass provender in the inn, he espied his money; for, behold, it *was* in his sack's mouth. ²⁸And he said unto his brethren, My money is restored; and, lo, *it is* even in my sack: and their heart failed *them,* and they were afraid, saying one to another, What *is* this *that* _____ hath done unto us?

²⁹And they came unto Jacob their father unto the land of Canaan, and told him all that befell unto them; saying, ³⁰The man, *who is* the lord of the land, spake roughly to us, and took us for spies of the country. ³¹And we said unto him, We *are* true *men;* we are no spies: ³²We *be* twelve brethren, sons of our father; one *is* not, and the youngest *is* this day with our father in the land of Canaan. ³³And the man, the lord of the country, said unto us, Hereby shall I know that ye *are* true *men;* leave one of your brethren *here* with me, and take *food for* the famine of your households, and be gone: ³⁴And bring your youngest brother unto me: then shall I know that ye *are* no spies, but *that* ye *are* true *men: so* will I deliver you your brother, and ye shall traffick in the land.

³⁵And it came to pass as they emptied their sacks, that, behold, every man's bundle of money *was* in his sack: and when *both* they and their father saw the bundles of money, they were afraid. ³⁶And Jacob their father said unto them, Me have ye bereaved *of my* children: _____ *is* not, and _____ *is* not, and ye will take _____ *away:* all these things are against me. ³⁷And _____ spake unto his father, saying, Slay my two sons, if I bring him not to thee: deliver him into my hand, and I will bring him to thee again. ³⁸And he said, My son shall not go down with you; for his brother is dead, and he is left alone: if mischief befall him by the way in the which ye go, then shall ye bring down my gray hairs with sorrow to the grave.

⁴³:¹And the famine *was* sore in the land. ²And it came to pass, when they had eaten up the corn which they had brought out of Egypt, their father said unto them, Go again, buy us a little food. ³And Judah spake unto him, saying, The man did solemnly protest unto us, saying, Ye shall not see my face, except your brother *be* with you. ⁴If thou wilt send our brother with us, we will go down and buy thee food: ⁵But if thou wilt not send *him,* we will not go down: for the man said unto us, Ye shall not see my face, except your brother *be* with you. ⁶And Israel said, Wherefore dealt ye so ill with me, as to tell the man whether ye had yet a brother? ⁷And they said, The man asked us straitly of our state, and of our kindred, saying, *Is* your father yet alive? have ye *another* brother? and we told him according to the tenor of these words: could we certainly know that he would say, Bring your brother down? ⁸And _____ said unto Israel his father, Send the lad with me, and

we will arise and go; that we may live, and not die, both we, and thou, *and* also our little ones. ⁹I will be surety for him; of my hand shalt thou require him: if I bring him not unto thee, and set him before thee, then let me bear the blame for ever: ¹⁰For except we had lingered, surely now we had returned this second time. ¹¹And their father Israel said unto them, If *it must be* so now, do this; take of the best fruits in the land in your vessels, and carry down the man a present, a little balm, and a little honey, spices, and myrrh, nuts, and almonds: ¹²And take double money in your hand; and the money that was brought again in the mouth of your sacks, carry *it* again in your hand; peradventure it *was* an

_____ : ¹³Take also your brother, and arise, go again unto the man: ¹⁴And God Almighty give you mercy before the man, that he may send away your other brother, and Benjamin. If I be bereaved *of my children,* I am bereaved.

¹⁵And the men took that present, and they took double money in their hand, and Benjamin; and rose up, and went down to Egypt, and stood before Joseph. ¹⁶And when Joseph saw Benjamin with them, he said to the ruler of his house, Bring *these* men home, and slay, and make ready; for *these* men shall dine with me at noon. ¹⁷And the man did as Joseph bade; and the man brought the men into Joseph's house. ¹⁸And the men were afraid, because they were brought into Joseph's house; and they said, Because of the money that was returned in our sacks at the first time are we brought in; that he may seek occasion against us, and fall upon us, and take us for bondmen, and our asses. ¹⁹And they came near to the steward of Joseph's house, and they communed with him at the door of the house, ²⁰And said, O sir, we came indeed down at the first time to buy food: ²¹And it came to pass, when we came to the inn, that we opened our sacks, and, behold, *every* man's money *was* in the mouth of his sack, our money in full weight: and we have brought it again in our hand. ²²And other money have we brought down in our hands to buy food: we cannot tell who put our money in our sacks. ²³And he said, Peace *be* to you, fear not: your _____ , and the God of your _____ , hath given you _____ in your _____ : I had your money. And he brought Simeon out unto them. ²⁴And the man brought the men into Joseph's house, and gave *them* water, and they washed their feet; and he gave their asses provender. ²⁵And they made ready the present against Joseph came at noon: for they heard that they should eat bread there.

²⁶And when Joseph came home, they brought him the present which *was* in their hand into the house, and bowed themselves to him to the earth. ²⁷And he asked them of *their* welfare, and said, *Is* your father well, the old man of whom ye spake? *Is* he yet alive? ²⁸And they answered, Thy servant our father *is* in good health, he *is* yet alive. And they bowed down their heads, and made _____ . ²⁹And he lifted up his eyes, and saw his brother Benjamin, his mother's son, and said, *Is* this your younger brother, of whom ye spake unto me? And he said, God be gracious unto thee, my son. ³⁰And Joseph made haste; for his bowels did yearn upon his brother: and he sought *where* to weep; and he entered into *his* chamber, and wept there. ³¹And he washed his face, and went out, and refrained himself, and said, Set on bread. ³²And they set on for him by himself, and for them by themselves, and for the Egyptians, which did eat with him, by themselves: because the Egyptians might not eat bread with the Hebrews; for that *is* an abomination unto the Egyptians. ³³And they sat before him, the firstborn according to his birthright, and the youngest according to his youth: and the men marvelled one at another. ³⁴And he took *and sent* messes unto them from before him: but Benjamin's mess was five times so much as any of theirs. And they drank, and were merry with him.

44:1And he commanded the steward of his house, saying, Fill the men's sacks *with* food, as much as they can carry, and put every man's money in his sack's mouth. 2And put my cup, the silver cup, in the sack's mouth of the youngest, and his corn money. And he did according to the word that Joseph had spoken. 3As soon as the morning was light, the men were sent away, they and their asses. 4*And* when they were gone out of the city, *and* not *yet* far off, Joseph said unto his steward, Up, follow after the men; and when thou dost overtake them, say unto them, Wherefore have ye rewarded evil for good? 5*Is* not this *it* in which my lord drinketh, and whereby indeed he _____? ye have done evil in so doing.

6And he overtook them, and he spake unto them these same words. 7And they said unto him, Wherefore saith my lord these words? God forbid that thy servants should do according to this thing: 8Behold, the money, which we found in our sacks' mouths, we brought again unto thee out of the land of Canaan: how then should we steal out of thy lord's house silver or gold? 9With whomsoever of thy servants it be found, both let him die, and we also will be my lord's bondmen. 10And he said, Now also *let* it *be* according unto your words; he with whom it is found shall be my servant; and ye shall be blameless. 11Then they speedily took down every man his sack to the ground, and opened every man his sack. 12And he searched, *and* began at the eldest, and left at the youngest: and the cup was found in Benjamin's sack. 13Then they rent their clothes, and laded every man his ass, and returned to the city.

14And Judah and his brethren came to Joseph's house; for he *was* yet there: and they fell before him on the ground. 15And Joseph said unto them, What deed *is* this that ye have done? wot ye not that such a man as I can certainly divine? 16And Judah said, What shall we say unto my lord? what shall we speak? or how shall we clear ourselves? _____ hath _____ out the _____ of thy _____: behold, we *are* my lord's servants, both we, and *he* also with whom the cup is found. 17And he said, God forbid that I should do so: *but* the man in whose hand the cup is found, he shall be my servant; and as for you, get you up in peace unto your father.

18Then Judah came near unto him, and said, Oh my lord, let thy servant, I pray thee, speak a word in my lord's ears, and let not thine anger burn against thy servant: for thou *art* even as Pharaoh. 19My lord asked his servants, saying, Have ye a father, or a brother? 20And we said unto my lord, We have a father, an old man, and a child of his old age, a little one; and his brother is dead, and he alone is left of his mother, and his father loveth him. 21And thou saidst unto thy servants, Bring him down unto me, that I may set mine eyes upon him. 22And we said unto my lord, The lad cannot leave his father: for *if* he should leave his father, *his father* would die. 23And thou saidst unto thy servants, Except your youngest brother come down with you, ye shall see my face no more. 24And it came to pass when we came up unto thy servant my father, we told him the words of my lord. 25And our father said, Go again, *and* buy us a little food. 26And we said, We cannot go down: if our youngest brother be with us, then will we go down: for we may not see the man's face, except our youngest brother *be* with us. 27And thy servant my father said unto us, Ye know that my wife bare me two *sons:* 28And the one went out from me, and I said, Surely he is torn in pieces; and I saw him not since: 29And if ye take this also from me, and mischief befall him, ye shall bring down my gray hairs with sorrow to the grave. 30Now therefore when I come to thy servant my father, and the lad *be* not with us; seeing that his life is bound up in the lad's life; 31It shall come to pass, when he seeth that the lad *is* not *with us,* that he will die: and thy servants shall bring down the gray hairs of thy servant our father with sorrow to the grave. ³²For thy servant became surety for the lad unto my father, saying, If I bring him not unto thee, then I shall bear the blame to my father for ever. ³³Now therefore, I pray thee, let thy servant abide instead of the lad a bondman to my lord; and let the lad go up with his brethren. ³⁴For how shall I go up to my father, and the lad *be* not with me? lest peradventure I see the evil that shall come on my father.

⁴⁵:¹Then Joseph could not refrain himself before all them that stood by him; and he cried, Cause every man to go out from me. And there stood no man with him, while Joseph made himself _____ unto his brethren. ²And he wept aloud: and the Egyptians and the house of Pharaoh heard. ³And Joseph said unto his brethren, I *am* _____; doth my father yet live? And his brethren could not answer him; for they were troubled at his presence. ⁴And Joseph said unto his brethren, Come near to me, I pray you. And they came near. And he said, I *am* Joseph your _____, whom ye sold into Egypt. ⁵Now therefore be not grieved, nor angry with yourselves, that ye sold me hither: for _____ did _____ me before you to _____ life. ⁶For these two years *hath* the famine *been* in the land: and yet *there are* five years, in the which *there shall* neither *be* earing nor harvest. ⁷And God sent me before you to _____ you a _____ in the earth, and to save your lives by a great deliverance. ⁸So now *it was* _____ you *that* sent me hither, but _____: and he hath made me a father to Pharaoh, and lord of all his house, and a ruler throughout all the land of Egypt. ⁹Haste ye, and go up to my father, and say unto him, Thus saith thy son Joseph, God hath made me lord of all Egypt: come down unto me, tarry not: ¹⁰And thou shalt dwell in the land of _____, and thou shalt be near unto me, thou, and thy children, and thy children's children, and thy flocks, and thy herds, and all that thou hast: ¹¹And there will I nourish thee; for yet *there are* five years of famine; lest thou, and thy household, and all that thou hast, come to poverty. ¹²And, behold, your eyes see, and the eyes of my brother Benjamin, that *it is* my mouth that speaketh unto you. ¹³And ye shall tell my father of all my glory in Egypt, and of all that ye have seen; and ye shall haste and bring down my father hither. ¹⁴And he fell upon his brother Benjamin's neck, and wept; and Benjamin wept upon his neck. ¹⁵Moreover he kissed all his brethren, and wept upon them: and after that his brethren talked with him.

¹⁶And the fame thereof was heard in Pharaoh's house, saying, Joseph's brethren are come: and it pleased Pharaoh well, and his servants. ¹⁷And Pharaoh said unto Joseph, Say unto thy brethren, This do ye; lade your beasts, and go, get you unto the land of Canaan; ¹⁸And take your father and your households, and come unto me: and I will give you the good of the land of Egypt, and ye shall eat the fat of the land. ¹⁹Now thou art commanded, this do ye; take you wagons out of the land of Egypt for your little ones, and for your wives, and bring your father, and come. ²⁰Also regard not your stuff; for the good of all the land of Egypt *is* yours. ²¹And the children of Israel did so: and Joseph gave them wagons, according to the commandment of Pharaoh, and gave them provision for the way. ²²To all of them he gave each man changes of raiment; but to Benjamin he gave three hundred *pieces* of silver, and five changes of raiment. ²³And to his father he sent after this *manner;* ten asses laden with the good things of Egypt, and ten she asses laden with corn and bread and meat for his father by the way. ²⁴So he sent his brethren away, and they departed: and he said unto them, See that ye fall not out by the way.

25And they went up out of Egypt, and came into the land of Canaan unto Jacob their father, 26And told him, saying, Joseph *is* yet alive, and he *is* governor over all the land of Egypt. And Jacob's heart fainted, for he believed them not. 27And they told him all the words of Joseph, which he had said unto them: and when he saw the wagons which Joseph had sent to carry him, the spirit of Jacob their father revived: 28And Israel said, *It is* enough; Joseph my son *is* yet alive: I will go and see him before I die.

46:1And Israel took his journey with all that he had, and came to Beer-sheba, and offered sacrifices unto the God of his father Isaac. 2And God spake unto Israel in the visions of the night, and said, _____, _____. And he said, Here *am* I. 3And he said, I *am* _____, the God of thy father: fear not to go down into Egypt; for I will there make of thee a great nation: 4I will go down with thee into Egypt; and I will also surely bring thee up *again:* and Joseph shall put his hand upon thine eyes. 5And Jacob rose up from Beer-sheba: and the sons of Israel carried Jacob their father, and their little ones, and their wives, in the wagons which Pharaoh had sent to carry him. 6And they took their cattle, and their goods, which they had gotten in the land of Canaan, and came into Egypt, Jacob, and all his seed with him: 7His sons, and his sons' sons with him, his daughters, and his sons' daughters, and all his seed brought he with him into Egypt.

8And these *are* the names of the children of Israel, which came into Egypt, Jacob and his sons: Reuben, Jacob's firstborn. 9And the sons of Reuben; Hanoch, and Phallu, and Hezron, and Carmi.

10And the sons of Simeon; Jemuel, and Jamin, and Ohad, and Jachin, and Zohar, and Shaul the son of a Canaanitish woman.

11And the sons of Levi; Gershon, Kohath, and Merari.

12And the sons of Judah; Er, and Onan, and Shelah, and Pharez, and Zarah: but Er and Onan died in the land of Canaan. And the sons of Pharez were Hezron and Hamul.

13And the sons of Issachar; Tola, and Phuvah, and Job, and Shimron.

14And the sons of Zebulun; Sered, and Elon, and Jahleel. 15These *be* the sons of Leah, which she bare unto Jacob in Padan-aram, with his daughter Dinah: all the souls of his sons and his daughters *were* thirty and three.

16And the sons of Gad; Ziphion, and Haggi, Shuni, and Ezbon, Eri, and Arodi, and Areli.

17And the sons of Asher; Jimnah, and Ishuah, and Isui, and Beriah, and Serah their sister: and the sons of Beriah; Heber, and Malchiel. 18These *are* the sons of Zilpah, whom Laban gave to Leah his daughter, and these she bare unto Jacob, *even* sixteen souls. 19The sons of Rachel Jacob's wife; Joseph, and Benjamin.

20And unto Joseph in the land of Egypt were born Manasseh and Ephraim, which Asenath the daughter of Poti-pherah priest of On bare unto him.

21And the sons of Benjamin were Belah, and Becher, and Ashbel, Gera, and Naaman, Ehi, and Rosh, Muppim, and Huppim, and Ard. 22These *are* the sons of Rachel, which were born to Jacob: all the souls *were* fourteen.

23And the sons of Dan; Hushim.

24And the sons of Naphtali; Jahzeel, and Guni, and Jezer, and Shillem. 25These *are* the sons of Bilhah, which Laban gave unto Rachel his daughter, and she bare these unto Jacob: all the souls *were* seven. 26All the souls that came with Jacob into Egypt, which came out of his loins, besides Jacob's sons' wives, all the souls *were* _____ and

_____ ; ²⁷And the sons of Joseph, which were born him in Egypt, *were* two souls: all the souls of the house of Jacob, which came into Egypt, *were* _____ and _____ .

²⁸And he sent Judah before him unto Joseph, to direct his face unto _____ ; and they came into the land of Goshen. ²⁹And Joseph made ready his chariot, and went up to meet Israel his father, to Goshen, and presented himself unto him; and he fell on his neck, and wept on his neck a good while. ³⁰And Israel said unto Joseph, Now let me die, since I have seen thy face, because thou *art* yet alive. ³¹And Joseph said unto his brethren, and unto his father's house, I will go up, and shew Pharaoh, and say unto him, My brethren, and my father's house, which *were* in the land of Canaan, are come unto me; ³²And the men *are* _____ , for their trade hath been to feed cattle; and they have brought their flocks, and their herds, and all that they have. ³³And it shall come to pass, when Pharaoh shall call you, and shall say, What *is* your occupation? ³⁴That ye shall say, Thy servants' trade hath been about cattle from our youth even until now, both we, *and* also our fathers: that ye may dwell in the land of Goshen; for every _____ *is* an _____ unto the

_____ .

^{47:1}Then Joseph came and told Pharaoh, and said, My father and my brethren, and their flocks, and their herds, and all that they have, are come out of the land of Canaan; and, behold, they *are* in the land of Goshen. ²And he took some of his brethren, *even* five men, and presented them unto Pharaoh. ³And Pharaoh said unto his brethren, What *is* your occupation? And they said unto Pharaoh, Thy servants *are* shepherds, both we, *and* also our fathers. ⁴They said moreover unto Pharaoh, For to sojourn in the land are we come; for thy servants have no pasture for their flocks; for the famine *is* sore in the land of Canaan: now therefore, we pray thee, let thy servants dwell in the land of Goshen. ⁵And Pharaoh spake unto Joseph, saying, Thy father and thy brethren are come unto thee: ⁶The land of Egypt *is* before thee; in the best of the land make thy father and brethren to dwell; in the land of Goshen let them dwell: and if thou knowest *any* men of activity among them, then make them rulers over my cattle. ⁷And Joseph brought in Jacob his father, and set him before Pharaoh: and Jacob blessed Pharaoh. ⁸And Pharaoh said unto Jacob, How old *art* thou? ⁹And Jacob said unto Pharaoh, The days of the years of my pilgrimage *are* an hundred and thirty years: few and evil have the days of the years of my life been, and have not attained unto the days of the years of the life of my fathers in the days of their pilgrimage. ¹⁰And Jacob blessed Pharaoh, and went out from before Pharaoh.

¹¹And Joseph placed his father and his brethren, and gave them a possession in the land of Egypt, in the best of the land, in the land of Rameses, as Pharaoh had commanded. ¹²And Joseph nourished his father, and his brethren, and all his father's household, with bread, according to *their* families.

¹³And *there was* no bread in all the land; for the famine *was* very sore, so that the land of Egypt and *all* the land of Canaan fainted by reason of the famine. ¹⁴And Joseph gathered up all the money that was found in the land of Egypt, and in the land of Canaan, for the corn which they bought: and Joseph brought the money into Pharaoh's house. ¹⁵And when money failed in the land of Egypt, and in the land of Canaan, all the Egyptians came unto Joseph, and said, Give us bread: for why should we die in thy presence? for the money faileth. ¹⁶And Joseph said, Give your cattle; and I will give you for your cattle, if money fail. ¹⁷And they brought their cattle unto Joseph: and Joseph gave them bread *in exchange* for horses, and for the flocks, and for the cattle of the herds, and for the asses: and he fed them with bread for all their cattle for that year. ¹⁸When that

year was ended, they came unto him the second year, and said unto him, We will not hide *it* from my lord, how that our money is spent; my lord also hath our herds of cattle; there is not ought left in the sight of my lord, but our bodies, and our lands: ¹⁹Wherefore shall we die before thine eyes, both we and our land? buy us and our land for bread, and we and our land will be servants unto Pharaoh: and give *us* seed, that we may live, and not die, that the land be not desolate. ²⁰And Joseph bought all the land of Egypt for Pharaoh; for the Egyptians sold every man his field, because the famine prevailed over them: so the land became Pharaoh's. ²¹And as for the people, he removed them to cities from *one* end of the borders of Egypt even to the *other* end thereof. ²²Only the land of the priests bought he not; for the priests had a portion *assigned them* of Pharaoh, and did eat their portion which Pharaoh gave them: wherefore they sold not their lands. ²³Then Joseph said unto the people, Behold, I have bought you this day and your land for Pharaoh: lo, *here is* seed for you, and ye shall sow the land. ²⁴And it shall come to pass in the increase, that ye shall give the fifth *part* unto Pharaoh, and four parts shall be your own, for seed of the field, and for your food, and for them of your households, and for food for your little ones. ²⁵And they said, Thou hast saved our lives: let us find grace in the sight of my lord, and we will be Pharaoh's servants. ²⁶And Joseph made it a law over the land of Egypt unto this day, *that* Pharaoh should have the _____part; except the land of the priests only, *which* became not Pharaoh's.

²⁷And Israel dwelt in the land of Egypt, in the country of Goshen; and they had possessions therein, and grew, and multiplied exceedingly. ²⁸And Jacob lived in the land of Egypt seventeen years: so the whole age of Jacob was an hundred forty and seven years. ²⁹And the time drew nigh that Israel must die: and he called his son Joseph, and said unto him, If now I have found grace in thy sight, put, I pray thee, thy hand under my thigh, and deal kindly and truly with me; bury me _____, I pray thee, in _____: ³⁰But I will lie with my fathers, and thou shalt carry me out of Egypt, and bury me in their buryingplace. And he said, I will do as thou hast said. ³¹And he said, Swear unto me. And he sware unto him. And Israel bowed himself upon the bed's head.

⁴⁸:¹And it came to pass after these things, that *one* told Joseph, Behold, thy father *is* sick: and he took with him his two sons, Manasseh and Ephraim. ²And *one* told Jacob, and said, Behold, thy son Joseph cometh unto thee: and Israel strengthened himself, and _____upon the bed. ³And Jacob said unto Joseph, God Almighty appeared unto me at Luz in the land of Canaan, and blessed me, ⁴And said unto me, Behold, I will make thee fruitful, and multiply thee, and I will make of thee a multitude of people; and will give this land to thy seed after thee *for* an everlasting possession.

⁵And now thy two sons, Ephraim and Manasseh, which were born unto thee in the land of Egypt before I came unto thee into Egypt, *are* _____; as Reuben and Simeon, they shall be mine. ⁶And thy issue, which thou begettest after them, shall be thine, *and* shall be called after the name of their brethren in their inheritance. ⁷And as for me, when I came from Padan, Rachel died by me in the land of Canaan in the way, when yet *there was* but a little way to come unto Ephrath: and I buried her there in the way of Ephrath; the same is _____. ⁸And Israel beheld Joseph's sons, and said, Who *are* these? ⁹And Joseph said unto his father, They *are* my sons, whom God hath given me in this *place.* And he said, Bring them, I pray thee, unto me, and I will bless them. ¹⁰Now the eyes of Israel were dim for age, *so that* he could not see. And he brought them near unto him; and he kissed them, and embraced them. ¹¹And Israel said unto Joseph, I had not thought to see

thy face: and, lo, God hath shewed me also thy seed. [12]And Joseph brought them out from between his knees, and he bowed himself with his face to the earth. [13]And Joseph took them both, Ephraim in his right hand toward Israel's left hand, and Manasseh in his left hand toward Israel's right hand, and brought *them* near unto him. [14]And Israel stretched out his _____hand, and laid it upon _____head, who *was* the _____, and his _____ hand upon _____head, guiding his hands _____; for Manasseh *was* the _____.

[15]And he blessed Joseph, and said, God, before whom my fathers Abraham and Isaac did walk, the God which fed me all my life long unto this day, [16]The _____which _____ me from all evil, bless the lads; and let my name be named on them, and the name of my fathers Abraham and Isaac; and let them grow into a multitude in the midst of the earth. [17]And when Joseph saw that his father laid his right hand upon the head of Ephraim, it displeased him: and he held up his father's hand, to remove it from Ephraim's head unto Manasseh's head. [18]And Joseph said unto his father, Not so, my father: for this *is* the firstborn; put thy right hand upon his head. [19]And his father _____, and said, I _____ *it,* my son, I _____ *it:* he also shall become a people, and he also shall be great: but truly his younger brother shall be _____than he, and his seed shall become a multitude of nations. [20]And he blessed them that day, saying, In thee shall Israel bless, saying, God make thee as Ephraim and as Manasseh: and he set Ephraim before Manasseh. [21]And Israel said unto Joseph, Behold, I die: but God shall be with you, and bring you again unto the land of your fathers. [22]Moreover I have given to thee one portion above thy brethren, which I took out of the hand of the Amorite with my _____and with my _____.

[49:1]And Jacob called unto his sons, and said, Gather yourselves together, that I may tell you *that* which shall befall you in the last days. [2]Gather yourselves together, and hear, ye sons of Jacob; and hearken unto Israel your father.

[3] _____, thou *art* my firstborn, my might, and the beginning of my strength, the excellency of dignity, and the excellency of power: [4]Unstable as water, thou shalt not excel; because thou wentest up to thy father's bed; then defiledst thou *it:* he went up to my couch.

[5] _____ and _____*are* brethren; instruments of cruelty *are in* their habitations. [6]O my soul, come not thou into their secret; unto their assembly, mine honour, be not thou united: for in their _____they slew a man, and in their _____they digged down a wall. [7]Cursed *be* their _____, for *it was* fierce; and their wrath, for it was _____: I will divide them in Jacob, and scatter them in Israel.

[8] _____, thou *art he* whom thy brethren shall _____: thy hand *shall be* in the neck of thine enemies; thy father's children shall bow down before thee. [9]Judah *is* a _____whelp: from the prey, my son, thou art gone up: he stooped down, he couched as a lion, and as an old lion; who shall rouse him up? [10]The _____shall not depart from Judah, nor a law_____giver from between his feet, until _____come; and unto him *shall* the gathering of the people *be.* [11]Binding his foal unto the vine, and his ass's colt unto the choice vine; he washed his garments in wine, and his clothes in the blood of grapes: [12]His eyes *shall be* red with wine, and his teeth white with milk.

[13] _____shall dwell at the haven of the sea; and he *shall be* for an haven of ships; and his border *shall be* unto _____.

14_____ *is* a strong ass couching down between two burdens: ¹⁵And he saw that rest *was* good, and the land that *it was* pleasant; and bowed his shoulder to bear, and became a servant unto tribute.

16_____ shall judge his people, as one of the tribes of Israel. ¹⁷Dan shall be a serpent by the way, an adder in the path, that biteth the horse heels, so that his rider shall fall backward. ¹⁸I have waited for thy _____, O LORD.

19_____, a troop shall overcome him: but he shall overcome at the last.

²⁰Out of _____ his bread *shall be* fat, and he shall yield royal dainties.

21_____ *is* a hind let loose: he giveth goodly words.

22_____ *is* a fruitful b_____ough, *even* a fruitful bough by a _____; *whose* branches run over the wall: ²³The archers have sorely grieved him, and shot *at him,* and hated him: ²⁴But his bow abode in strength, and the arms of his hands were made strong by the hands of the mighty *God* of Jacob; (from thence *is* the _____, the _____ of Israel:) ²⁵*Even* by the God of thy father, who shall _____ thee; and by the Almighty, who shall _____ thee with blessings of heaven above, blessings of the deep that lieth under, blessings of the breasts, and of the womb: ²⁶The blessings of thy father have prevailed above the blessings of my progenitors unto the utmost bound of the everlasting hills: they shall be on the head of Joseph, and on the crown of the head of him that was separate from his brethren.

27_____ shall ravin *as* a wolf: in the morning he shall devour the prey, and at night he shall divide the spoil.

²⁸All these *are* the twelve tribes of Israel: and this *is it* that their father spake unto them, and blessed them; every one according to his blessing he blessed them. ²⁹And he charged them, and said unto them, I am to be gathered unto my people: bury me with my fathers in the cave that *is* in the field of Ephron the Hittite, ³⁰In the cave that *is* in the field of Machpelah, which *is* before Mamre, in the land of Canaan, which Abraham bought with the field of Ephron the Hittite for a possession of a buryingplace. ³¹There they buried Abraham and Sarah his wife; there they buried Isaac and Rebekah his wife; and there I buried Leah. ³²The purchase of the field and of the cave that *is* therein *was* from the children of Heth. ³³And when Jacob had made an end of commanding his sons, he gathered up his feet into the bed, and yielded up the ghost, and was gathered unto his people.

^{50:1}And Joseph fell upon his father's face, and wept upon him, and kissed him. ²And Joseph commanded his servants the physicians to _____ his father: and the physicians embalmed Israel. ³And _____ days were fulfilled for him; for so are fulfilled the days of those which are _____: and the Egyptians mourned for him threescore and ten days. ⁴And when the days of his mourning were past, Joseph spake unto the house of Pharaoh, saying, If now I have found grace in your eyes, speak, I pray you, in the ears of Pharaoh, saying, ⁵My father made me swear, saying, Lo, I die: in my grave which I have digged for me in the land of Canaan, there shalt thou bury me. Now therefore let me go up, I pray thee, and bury my father, and I will come again. ⁶And Pharaoh said, Go up, and bury thy father, according as he made thee swear.

⁷And Joseph went up to bury his father: and with him went up all the servants of Pharaoh, the elders of his house, and all the elders of the land of Egypt, ⁸And all the house of Joseph, and his brethren, and his father's house: only their little ones, and their flocks, and their herds, they left in the land of Goshen. ⁹And there went up with him both

chariots and horsemen: and it was a very great company. ¹⁰And they came to the threshingfloor of Atad, which *is* beyond Jordan, and there they mourned with a great and very sore lamentation: and he made a mourning for his father seven days. ¹¹And when the inhabitants of the land, the Canaanites, saw the mourning in the floor of Atad, they said, This *is* a grievous mourning to the Egyptians: wherefore the name of it was called Abel-mizraim, which *is* beyond Jordan. ¹²And his sons did unto him according as he commanded them: ¹³For his sons carried him into the land of Canaan, and buried him in the cave of the field of Machpelah, which Abraham bought with the field for a possession of a buryingplace of Ephron the Hittite, before Mamre.

¹⁴And Joseph returned into Egypt, he, and his brethren, and all that went up with him to bury his father, after he had buried his father.

¹⁵And when Joseph's brethren saw that their father was dead, they said, Joseph will peradventure hate us, and will certainly requite us all the evil which we did unto him. ¹⁶And they sent a messenger unto Joseph, saying, Thy father did command before he died, saying, ¹⁷So shall ye say unto Joseph, _____, I pray thee now, the trespass of thy brethren, and their sin; for they did unto thee _____: and now, we pray thee, _____ the trespass of the servants of the God of thy father. And Joseph wept when they spake unto him. ¹⁸And his brethren also went and fell down before his face; and they said, Behold, we *be* thy servants. ¹⁹And Joseph said unto them, _____: for *am* I in the place of God? ²⁰But as for you, ye thought _____against me; *but* _____meant it unto _____, to bring to pass, as *it is* this day, to _____much people alive. ²¹Now therefore fear ye not: I will nourish you, and your little ones. And he comforted them, and spake kindly unto them.

²²And Joseph dwelt in Egypt, he, and his father's house: and Joseph lived an hundred and ten years. ²³And Joseph saw Ephraim's children of the third *generation:* the children also of Machir the son Manasseh were brought up upon Joseph's knees. ²⁴And Joseph said unto his brethren, I die: and God will surely visit you, and bring you out of this land unto the land which he sware to Abraham, to Isaac, and to Jacob. ²⁵And Joseph took an oath of the children of Israel, saying, God will surely visit you, and ye shall carry up my _____from hence. ²⁶So Joseph died, *being* an hundred and ten years old: and they _____him, and he was put in a _____in _____.

Made in the USA
Columbia, SC
26 March 2025

55706455R00030